DEMCO 38-297

DATE DUE

D1071273

ROBERT SILVERBERG

PS 3569 .I472 Z6 1983
Clareson, Thomas D.
Robert Silverberg

STARMONT READER'S GUIDE 18

THOMAS D. CLARESON

Series Editor: Roger C. Schlobin

R. Reginald

the Borgo Press

San Bernardino, California
MCMLXXXIV

RITTER LIBRARY
BALDWIN - WALLACE COLLEGE

ABBREVIATIONS

ABY—*Across a Billion Years*
B1—*The Best of Robert Silverberg, Vol. 1*
B2—*The Best of Robert Silverberg, Vol. 2*
CP—*Capricorn Games*
F&SF—*The Magazine of Fantasy & Science Fiction*
MM—*The Man in the Maze*
MT—*The Masks of Time*
SB—"Sounding Brass, Tinkling Cymbal"
SFA—*Science Fiction Adventures*
SFQ—*Science Fiction Quarterly*
SSF—*Super-Science Fiction*
UT—*Unfamiliar Territory*

Library of Congress Cataloging in Publication Data:

Clareson, Thomas D.
  Robert Silverberg.

  (Starmont reader's guide ; 18)
  Includes bibliographies and index.
  1. Silverberg, Robert--Criticism and interpretation. I. Title.
II. Series.
PS3569.I472Z6 1983   813'.54   83-542
ISBN 0-916732-48-7
ISBN 0-916732-47-9 (pbk.)

Copyright © 1983 by Starmont House.
All rights reserved. International copyrights reserved in all
countries. No part of this book may be reproduced in any form,
except for brief passages quoted in reviews, without written
permission of the publisher.

Published by Starmont House, P.O. Box 851, Mercer Island,
WA 98040, USA. Composition by The Borgo Press. Cover design
by Stephen E. Fabian.

First Edition———May, 1983

THOMAS D. CLARESON is the Founding Editor of *Extrapolation*,
the first journal devoted to science-fiction criticism. The author of
numerous books and articles, he currently is a Professor of English
at the College of Wooster, Wooster, Ohio.

CONTENTS

A NOTE ON THE TEXT

In preparing this work on Robert Silverberg—the first of this length—I have drawn upon a number of earlier articles I wrote on Silverberg. In all cases I have reworked and rewritten such material because the greater length of this study demanded a more detailed discussion of the various phases of his career. Either in the Annotated Secondary Bibliography or elsewhere in the notations, I have given proper citation to those articles. I have informed the various editors and publishers; my thanks to them for raising no objections, especially since several of the works are now out-of-print.

Regarding matters of bibliography, I have consulted the manuscript of my *Robert Silverberg: A Primary and Secondary Bibliography*, to be published by G.K. Hall & Co. early in 1983.

Perhaps the most important matter rises from what may seem a discrepancy. When Silverberg has referred to specific stories and novels, he has most often cited the dates of *composition*. Uniformly in this text I have cited the first American book publication, although on occasion I have made mention of the first magazine publication as well. The reader should thus be aware that many of the works—in the late 1960's and the early 1970's in particular—were written during a shorter period of time than the dates of publication indicate. I have tried to point this out in those cases in which I thought it important.

CHRONOLOGY

1935	Born January 15 in New York, the only son of Michael and Helen (Baim)Silverberg.
1949	Begins publication of the fanzine, *Starship*, becoming deeply involved in Fandom.
1954	First professional short story, "Gorgon Planet," published in the February issue of *Nebula Science Fiction* (British).
1955	First novel, *Revolt on Alpha C*, published by Thomas Y. Crowell; during the summer he lives in an apartment house on West 114th Street, where he begins to collaborate with a neighbor, Randall Garrett, using the pseudonym Robert Randall. His friendship with Harlan Ellison, who lives in the same apartment house, also begins.
1956	Graduates from Columbia University with a B.A. in Comparative Literature; on 26 August he marries Barbara H. Brown; at the 1956 Worldcon in New York City, he receives the Hugo as the "Best New Author" of 1955.
1957	*The 13th Immortal*. *Master of Life and Death*. *The Shrouded Planet* (with Randall Garrett).
1958	*Invisible Barriers* (as David Osborne). *Invaders from Earth*. *Starhaven* (as Ivar Jorgenson). *Lest We Forget Thee, Earth* (as Calvin M. Knox). *Stepsons of Terra*. *Aliens from Space* (as David Osborne).
1958-1959	Under the pseudonym Calvin M. Knox, he conducts the review column, "The Book-Space," for *Science Fiction Adventures* and "Readin' & Writin'" for *Original Science Fiction Stories*. As Robert Silverberg, he writes the review column, "Infinity's Choice," during the latter half of 1958.
1959	*The Dawning Light* (with Randall Garrett).

> *Starman's Quest.*
> *The Planet Killers.*

1960   *Lost Race of Mars* (named by the *New York Times* as one of the 100 best books for children of the year).
Treasures Beneath the Sea (his first non-fiction book).

1961   *Collision Course.*

1962   *Next Stop the Stars* (the first collection of short stories).
Recalled to Life.
The Seed of Earth.
Purchases the Fiorello LaGuardia mansion in New York City.

1963   *The Silent Invaders.*

1964   *One of Our Planetoids Is Missing* (as Calvin M. Knox).
Regan's Planet.
Time of the Great Freeze.
Godling, Go Home (short stories).

1964-1965 Under his own name, Silverberg writes the review column, "Spectroscope" for *Amazing* from April, 1964, through August, 1965, and "Fantasy Books" for *Fantastic* in the spring of 1965.

1965   "We, the Marauders" in *A Pair from Space*.
The Mask of Akhnaten (juvenile novel; the only non-science-fiction novel published under his own name).
To Worlds Beyond (short stories).
Conquerors from the Darkness.

1966   *Earthmen and Strangers* (first edited anthology).
Needle in a Timestack (short stories).
In June, Silverberg states that he "fell into a mysterious illness," which was diagnosed as "a sudden hyperactivity of the thyroid gland."

1967   *Planet of Death.*
Those Who Watch.
The Time Hoppers.
The Gate of Worlds.
To Open the Sky.
Thorns (the first of his novels to be nominated for the Nebula Award and the Hugo as the "Best Novel" of the year).

1967-1968 Silverberg served as President of the Science Fiction Writers of America.

1968   *The Masks of Time* (published in Britain in 1970 as *Vornan-19*).
Hawksbill Station (published in Britain in 1969 as *The Anvil of Time*).

1969   *The Calibrated Alligator* (short stories).
The Man in the Maze.

Three Survived.
Across a Billion Years.
Dimension Thirteen (short stories).
Up the Line.
Nightwings.
To Live Again.
"Nightwings" wins Hugo as "Best Novella" of the year (this is the first section of the novel).
"Passengers" wins the Nebula Award as "Best Short Story" of the year (originally published in Damon Knight's *Orbit 4*).

1970   *Parsecs and Parables* (short stories).
Downward to the Earth.
Tower of Glass.
The Cube Root of Uncertainty (short stories).
World's Fair, 1992.
A Robert Silverberg Omnibus (published in London, this volume includes *Master of Life and Death*, *Invaders from Earth*, and *The Time-Hoppers*).
Silverberg was Guest of Honor at the World Science Fiction Convention in Heidelberg.

1971   *A Time of Changes* wins the Nebula Award as "Best Novel" of the year.
Moonferns & Starsongs (short stories).
Son of Man.
The World Inside.
New Dimensions I (first of the series of anthologies for which Silverberg received high praise).
"Good News from the Vatican" wins the Nebula Award as the "Best Short Story" of the year (originally published in Terry Carr's *Universe I*).

1972   *The Book of Skulls.*
The Reality Trip (short stories).
The Second Trip.
Dying Inside.
By early spring the Silverbergs had moved from New York City to Oakland, California.

1973   *Valley Beyond Time* (short stories).
Earth's Other Shadow (short stories).
Unfamiliar Territory (short stories).

1974   *Born with the Dead* (three novellas).
Sundance (short stories).
"Born with the Dead" wins the Nebula Award as the "Best Novella" of the year (originally published in the May *F&SF* special Silverberg issue).

1975   *The Feast of St. Dionysus* (short stories).
Sunrise on Mercury (short stories).

The Stochastic Man.

Throughout the year—as early as an April conference at the University of Colorado-Denver—Silverberg announced that he was quitting the field of science fiction.

1976   *The Best of Robert Silverberg*, volume 1 (short stories).

Capricorn Games (short stories).

Shadrach in the Furnace.

1976-1978 In the spring of 1976, Silverberg began reviewing for *Odyssey*; by May, 1977, he had a column, "Books," in *Cosmos*. In 1978 he began another column not confined to reviewing, "Opinion," in *Galileo*. By 1981 that column had become a regular feature of *Amazing Stories*.

1978   *The Best of Robert Silverberg*, volume 2 (short stories).

1979   *The Songs of Summer* (short stories).

1980   *Lord Valentine's Castle.*

1981   *A Robert Silverberg Omnibus* (published in New York, this volume includes *The Man in the Maze*, *Nightwings*, and *Downward to the Earth*).

The Desert of Stolen Dreams.

In February the Eaton Conference at the University of California-Riverside gave Silverberg the Milford Award for being a distinguished editor.

1982   *Majipoor Chronicles* (short stories).

The World of a Thousand Colors (short stories).

1983   *Lord of Darkness.*

I

THE (SCIENCE) FICTION FACTORY: 1955 - 1959

No one now seriously questions the importance of the contribution made by Robert Silverberg, both as a writer and as an
editor, to contemporary science fiction during the last quarter
century. The main difficulty involving any general assessment of
his career to date rises from a twofold problem. First, during the
period 1955 through 1959, he was extremely productive, supposedly more so than at any other time. Secondly, the legend has been
widely accepted that he abandoned science fiction—perhaps
because the earliest criticism of his work was inconsistent—returning to it in the mid-1960's a distinctly different writer. It is one
that he himself has helped to foster in such an autobiographical
essay as "Sounding Brass, Tinkling Cymbal" (1975).

There he sketches a childhood that he chooses to call "a painful
time, lonely and embittering"—in part because he was a precocious only child. As a result, he asserts that the "lure of the
exotic seized me early." [1] In addition to hobbies and museums,
there was his reading: Verne, Wells, and Twain came early.
He also "dabbled in comic books," recalling "gaudy memories"
of Buck Rogers and *Planet Comics*, although he did not discover
Edgar Rice Burroughs. It wasn't until 1948 that he became
acquainted with the science-fiction magazines, but by the spring of
1949, he had begun to issue the fanzine, *Starship*, which plunged
him into fandom and led to his first professional publication when
he wrote "Fanmag" for *SFA* in December, 1953.

Earlier Donald A. Wollheim's *Portable Novels of Science*
"had enormous impact" on him because of four stories in particular: Wells's *First Men in the Moon*, Taine's *Before the Dawn*,
Lovecraft's *Shadow Out of Time*, and "above all" Stapledon's
Odd John. He had thought of a career as a journalist "while
writing science fiction as a sideline"; the field attracted him
because it "allowed me to give free play to those fantasies of
space and time and dinosaurs and supermen that were so grati-
fying to me." [2] He also mentioned his early fascination with
time travel.

His first professional story was "Gorgon Planet" in the British magazine *Nebula Science Fiction* in February, 1954. A month earlier he had sold a novel to Thomas Y. Crowell. Although he was asked to do extensive revision of the narrative—which led to a complete rewriting—*Revolt on Alpha C* was published in the summer of 1955. Floyd C. Gale thought that this tale of colonists revolting against Earth awakened in the young hero "an understanding of history that kids will excitedly share," but P. Schuyler Miller found it to be "precisely the kind of vague attitude toward just causes and underdogs that produced a lot of bewildered fellow-travelers for Communist front activities." Hans Stefan Santesson called the plot "interesting." [3]

By the summer of 1955, however, Silverberg's career had taken a dramatic turn. He lived in an apartment house on West 114th Street, where the established writer, Randall Garrett, was his next-door neighbor, and Harlan Ellison also had an apartment in the building. Although Garrett introduced the youthful Silverberg to various editors of science-fiction magazines, more importantly the two began to collaborate, using the name "Robert Randall." Silverberg has said that by the 1980's he can no longer always recall precisely who wrote what, but their first notable success was a trilogy of novellas done specifically for John W. Campbell's *Astounding* ("The Chosen People," June 1956; "The Promised Land," August 1956; "False Prophet," December 1956), which were reworked into the novel, *The Shrouded Planet*, published by Gnome Press in 1957. *The Dawning Light* followed: first serialized in *Astounding* in three parts (March through May, 1957) and then released by Gnome Press in 1959. Although the collaboration continued, Silverberg had begun to produce prolifically (he has spoken of "that early rush of energy" starting in the summer of 1955, [4] the first of several such periods). By the end of 1956 he had placed a million words in print, and pseudonyms—often "house names"—had already become a necessity because he sometimes had more than one story in a single issue of such magazines as *Amazing Stories*.

In June, 1956, he graduated from Columbia University, having majored in Comparative Literature. On August 26, 1956, he married Barbara H. Brown. The newlyweds went to Worldcon in New York City, where Silverberg received a Hugo Award as "Best New Writer" for 1955. From there, the couple went to the Milford Science Fiction Writers' Workshop held at Damon Knight's home in Milford, Pennsylvania.

At various times in conversation, he has explained that to live comfortably in New York, he had decided to write 50,000 words a month; even at a penny a word that would assure him of a monthly income of $500—a figure comparable at the time to the salaries received by his friends who had started work in one of the sciences or in engineering. "I developed a deadly facility," he wrote in

"Sounding Brass, Tinkling Cymbal"; "if an editor needed a 7500-word story of an alien conquest in three days, he need only phone me and I would produce it . . . . I was the complete writing machine, turning out stories in all lengths at whatever quality the editor desired, from slam-bang adventure to cerebral pseudo-philosophy . . . . I wanted to win economic security—to get enough money in the bank so that I would be insulated against the financial storms that had buffeted most of the writers I knew, some of the greatest in the field among them." [5]

Independently, between 1957 and 1959, eleven of his novels were published, most of them by Donald A. Wollheim in the Ace Doubles series, some of them under pseudonyms. During the same interval more than 220 of his stories appeared, at least half of which have never been reprinted. These numbers ignore the mystery stories and westerns, for example, which he churned out in those years—of which he does not now have a complete record—to say nothing of the more than one-hundred erotic novels he started publishing under the pseudonym Don Elliott/Eliot in 1959.

An enumeration of those novels gives some insight both into his methods and his variety. Anthony Boucher dismissed the first, *The 13th Immortal* (1957), as "a sketchy melodrama of palace-politics in a feudal post-atomic world," but he thought *Master of Life and Death* gave "a powerfully effective picture of a man of the year 2232 . . . [in] a world acting out the nightmares of Malthus." [6] Two aspects of the novel illustrate concerns which Silverberg was to pursue. The first is the theme of over-population; the second, the complexity of plotline. The early reviewers who praised him emphasized not only his skill as a storyteller but also his ability to create vivid, feasible backgrounds. "Thunder over Starhaven," a novella from *SFA* (October, 1957), became *Starhaven* (1958), the only book with which he used the pseudonym, Ivar Jorgenson, while "And the Walls Came Tumbling Down" (*If*, December 1957) grew into *Invisible Barriers* as David Osborne. The former portrays a world serving as a haven for outlaws of the universe, while the latter concerns efforts to thwart an impending alien invasion of Earth. *Lest We Forget Thee, Earth* (1958) combined three novellas from *SFA* ("Chalice of Death," June 1957; "Earth Shall Live Again," December 1957; "Vengeance of the Space Armada, March 1958) under the pseudonym Calvin M. Knox.

Although "We, the Marauders" (*SFQ*, February 1958) saw publication with James Blish's "Giants in the Earth" as *A Pair from Space* (1965), Silverberg had previously developed it into *Invaders from Earth* (1958), probably the most significant of his early novels. The narrative's point of departure rises out of the discovery by the Extraterrestrial Development and Exploration Corporation, Ganymede Division, that the moon is rich in needed radioactive materials. Deciding that it must take strong measures to protect its interests, the Corporation employs a public relations firm to persuade the citizens of Earth that the United Nations must underwrite the cost of a military occupation needed to subdue hostile aliens. The protagonist, Ted Kennedy, a member of the firm, creates an imaginary colony of three-hundred-and-thirteen persons, including women and children; then, he inundates the news media with falsified releases playing up the various sufferings of the supposed colonists. The scheme works, the public is enraged, but Kennedy is bothered by the hoax.

After he is sent to Ganymede to obtain local color intended to give his deception greater authenticity, Silverberg shifts the emphasis of the narrative so that *Invaders from Earth* becomes his most fully developed effort to date to explore man's reactions to an alien culture. Kennedy witnesses the brutality of the thirty-some Corporation men who are really the only humans on Ganymede. He is particularly appalled by the antagonism of the military officers towards the natives and anyone sympathetic to them. He learns that non-violence is the cornerstone of the aliens' philosophy. They accept stoically the harsh conditions of their world, trying to live as part of nature; they preach the need to respect all life—to understand the "currents of beingness." Kennedy learns that "the aliens are *people*; they provide a perspective from which to measure the conduct and nature of man; and they teach him what he has ignored or forgotten." [7] In terms of political and social criticism, if one were not aware of the publication date, the reader might easily think it one of his later novels—until the youthful Silverberg resolves all questions through a fast-moving plot. Ted Kennedy reveals the plot of the Corporation and is sent back to Ganymede as a special envoy of the United Nations. Although some short stories during the late 1950's make a similar use of the human-alien encounter, *Invaders from Earth* provides the most sustained, fully developed treatment of several of his subsequent themes.

Of the other novels of the period, both *Aliens from Space* (1958) as David Osborne and *The Plot Against the Earth* (1959) as Calvin M. Knox can be dismissed as "interstellar intrigue" of little consequence. [8] "This World Must Die" (*SFA*, August 1957) became *The Planet Killers* (1959), another adventure yarn.

As in the case of *Starman's Quest* (1959), one must recall that a number of these narratives were published for a juvenile audience. P. Schuyler Miller found this novel, dominated by a boy's search for a twin brother in a future New York, to be "a modern Alger-type story," although one sense that he implicitly disapproved of "the unlikely situation—in an old-time Alger book, at least—of a teen-ager setting out to become a successful gambler." [9] A second element of the plot involves the search for a lost space drive whose recovery will somehow solve the basic conflict of *Starman's Quest*: the antagonism between a small, elite group of spacers and the multitudes of a decadent Earth.

Originally the novella "Shadow on the Stars" (*SFA*, April 1958), the second most important of these early novels is *Stepsons of Terra* (1958). At first glance it could be judged as simply another one of a kind, for it deals with the threat of warfare with aliens. Projected late into the fourth millenium, the main plotline brings Baird Ewing to Earth as an emissary from the colony-planet, Corwin, to seek aid against the humanoid aliens, the Klodni, who completely devastate the planets which they briefly occupy. Although Earth has spawned a thousand colonies, the planet Corwin has had no contact with the mother-world for some five-hundred years. Thus, instead of a dynamic world capable of supplying Ewing with some super-weapon to destroy the galactic invaders, he finds an Earth that has become pacifist, not even possessing spaceships. Indeed Sirians (natives of the oldest colony-world, Sirius IV) are infiltrating Earth and obviously plan a coup.

Against this familiar science-fiction background, Silverberg achieves a noteworthy originality by developing what was to date his fullest treatment of time travel—"a theme that has always fascinated" him [10]—after Ewing encounters a group that possesses its secret. For a brief time, the time travel manipulations create four Ewings. More importantly, once he eliminates his alternative selves, he disposes of the Klodni by casting their fleet five million years into the past. Yet this narrative is no package neatly tied up by such a stunt, for Ewing returns to Earth to help the mother-world against the threat of the Sirians.

One notices immediately how many of these books grew out of novellas appearing in such magazines as *Science Fiction Adventures*. It was not a practice that ended in 1959. "Spawn of the Deadly Sea" (*SFA*, April 1957) was widely reviewed as *Conquerors from the Darkness* (1965), although many critics thought it essentially a sea-story adapted to a science-fiction background. [11] "Three Survived" (*SSF*, August 1957) saw book publication as *Three Survived* (1969). "Recalled to Life," a two-part serial in *Infinity* (June and August, 1958) explored the theme of immortality. Published in book form by Lancer in 1962, it was the one early novel which Silverberg extensively revised for a second edition (Doubleday, 1972).

The Silent Invaders (*Infinity*, October 1958; book form, 1963) again dealt with the theme of alien races, the Darruu and the Medlin, contending for control of Earth. Its significant innovation arises because its protagonist, Aar Khioom, a citizen of Darruu, has undergone surgery so that he can pass as the human, Major Abner Harris. He is planted on Earth to help manipulate public opinion; the main storyline involves his conversion to the Medlin cause. This is the earliest instance of such surgery; used very differently, it became a major device shaping such works as *Thorns* (1967), which figures prominently in what one may call the dark side of Silverberg's fiction.

In *Collision Course* (*Amazing*, July 1959; bookform, 1961) war threatens when humanity meets the Norglen, a race equally intent upon dominating the universe. A proposal to split the galaxy between the rivals comes to naught when mankind is coldly informed that it may retain only those worlds which it presently occupies; further Terran expansion is forbidden. The threat of open conflict is averted only after the discovery of a second race of aliens. They are so ancient and wise that they consider both Earthmen and Norglen mere "children."

All in all, counting the collaborations with Randall Garrett, twenty novels came out of the period 1955 through 1959. There were innumerable other novellas. Silverberg included a few in later collections, but most of them,usually written for such a magazine as *Science Fiction Adventures*, were never reprinted. They represent the hastily written stories of adventure to which Silverberg has referred, and their very titles call up the "pulp" tradition going back at least to the 1930's: "Battle for the Thousand Stars" (December 1956), "Lair of the Dragonbird" (December 1956), "Secret of the Green Invaders" (as Robert Randall, December 1956), "Slaves of the Star Giants" (February 1957), "The Flame and the Hammer" (September 1957), and "Valley Beyond Time" (December 1957), to name only some of the earliest. One senses a mixture of nostalgia and self-defense when Silverberg declared, "I had fun writing these melodramas of the spaceways, and the readers apparently enjoyed them too, for my stories (under whatever pseudonym) were usually the most popular offerings in each issue." [12] Undoubtedly, when Silverberg later reflected upon his earlier career, he felt some sense of guilt about the quantity of fiction that he had turned out so quickly and, perhaps, wished that he had followed the advice of friends and contemporaries who had, as early as the 1956 Milford Workshop, encouraged him to publish only his best work. In "Sounding Brass, Tinkling Cymbal," he remarked, " . . .I had served science fiction badly in my 1955-8 days . . . ." [13] He has explained that he withdrew from the science-fiction field when, in 1958, the market dried up. Yet one infers that a dissatisfaction with the quality of his fiction also contributed. One hears his growing reaction as early as the 1957 story, "En Route to Earth." An attractive young Vegan woman, Milissa, undertakes her first "extrasolar hop as a stewardess of the warp-liner *King Magnus*," during which she must take care of the mixed bag of aliens who are passengers. Of the story, which one of the characters is reading—

"Slaves of the Pink Beings"—she says, "It was typical science fiction, full of monsters and bloodshed, and just as dull as every other science fiction story she had tried to read." [14] He goes on to satirize fandom by having one alien offer the other a sizable amount of money for the "June 2114" issue of the unnamed magazine because he needs it for his collection.

This summary, however, does not yet tell the full story of Silverberg's career between 1955 and 1959. Although he was "seeking always the financial independence that I believed would free me from the karmic wheel of high-volume hackmanship," [15] he did write a number of quality stories that anticipated both the themes and the experiments with narrative technique characterizing his fiction of the late 1960's and 1970's. "The Songs of Summer" (1956), for example, makes use of fragmentary, overlapping monologues so that the reader can better understand the fate of the materialistic, aggressive Chester Dugan, cast from the present into an unspecified future in which mankind has returned to an essentially pastoral lifestyle and has the potential for telepathic unity.

Several times at least Silverberg has lamented that these stories did not readily sell. Perhaps the best-known incident involved "Road to Nightfall." Written in 1954, it found no market because editors thought it "depressing, morbid, negative"; [16] only after Harlan Ellison came to his aid and Hans Stefan Santesson became editor of *Fantastic Universe* did it see print in that magazine in 1958. Four years! That delay remains surprising because of the wave of post-atomic holocaust stories inundating the magazines after World War II, as represented by Theodore Sturgeon's "Thunder and Roses" (1947) and Judith Merril's "That Only a Mother" (1948), both published in Campbell's *Astounding*. Perhaps the difficulty lies in the lateness of the date, although by the mid-1950's, the dystopian view of the future had become an established part of modern science fiction; or again, many of the earlier cautionary tales of other writers (excepting such horror pieces as Merril's "That Only a Mother") "left some room for hope—perhaps for a rational decision which would prevent the extinction of civilization and mankind." [17] In contrast, "Road to Nightfall" reveals a destroyed America; New York, Trenton, and Baltimore have become oases in a radioactive desert. After food supplies from Trenton have been cut off, New York City faces starvation. Dogs are hunted for food; few individuals dare to go into the streets after dark or to venture into unknown neighborhoods. Katterson, the protagonist—a large man and an ex-soldier—refuses the offer made by Malory to recruit him as a hunter of meat. He similarly rejects the meat offered him by his mistress, a gift to her from an admirer. Yet, wracked by hunger, Katterson succumbs to cannibalism, as have his contemporaries.

He collapses on Malory's doorstep. The story becomes an important early example of the dark vision that permeated Silverberg's later fiction. Moveover, it can be read as a precursor to those tales of psychic cannibalism, such as "Warm Man" (*F&SF*, May 1957) and "The Winds of Siros" (*Venture*, September 1957), the latter of which he incorporated into the novel, *The Seed of Earth* (1962).

Silverberg also expanded "Hopper" (*Infinity*, October 1956) into the novel *The Time Hoppers* (1967), whose protagonist, Quellen, as an officer of the law, must first apprehend the individual who is sending persons into the past and then escapes from an over-populated twenty-fifth century by going back in time to pre-Columbian America. "The Man Who Never Forgot" (*F&SF*, February 1958) gains increased significance if one thinks of it as *Dying Inside* (1972) with a happy ending.

One should also examine some of the stories which Silverberg has repeatedly included in collections of his short fiction. Not only does such a sampling tell something about Silverberg's own evaluation of his work, but reveals that certain themes do recur, although the plotlines range across a wide spectrum. A few are humorous, but more turn upon some point of irony. One is frequently reminded of O. Henry in that the final line provides the narrative with a new twist—the reader with a new perspective. "The Old Man" (1957) serves as a good example. In an effective and sympathetic account of a spaceman's being forced into retirement, Silverberg leads to the revelation that the protagonist is not yet twenty. One senses, however, that although the stories all were well crafted, they remained mechanical exercises for Silverberg. There is none of the complex emotional involvement that the later stories and novels evoke.

"Collecting Team" (1956) convincingly reworks the old plot of a crew of Earthmen who are gathering fauna from an unknown world finding that they have been trapped and will become specimens in a zoo operated by unspecified aliens. "Birds of a Feather" (1958) is an exercise in con-artistry between Corrigan of "the Corrigan Institute of Morphological Science" (he has 690 specimens of 298 life forms in his sideshow) and Ildwar Gorb of the planet Wazzenazz XIII, who pretends to be an extraterrestrial in order to return to Earth. In a similar light vein, "A Man with Talent" (1956), Emil Vilar, flees from Earth where at best he can be a versifier instead of a poet; on Rigel Seven he discovers that the entire population is "omni-artistic" whereas he has but a single talent. Yet he is welcomed, for he will provide an audience.

Narrated in the first person by a son trained to be an historian, "There Was an Old Woman—" (1958) tells of the experiment of Donna Mitchell, a professor of Biochemistry, who irradiated a single zygote so that she produced—in her laboratory—thirty-one sons, all identical brothers (the thirty-second died before birth).

Believing that environment controls personality, she differentiated her sons at eighteen months, raised them on a farm in Wisconsin, educated them rigorously, and arbitrarily chose a profession for each. It is a highly individual treatment of the Frankenstein theme, for Professor Mitchell erred. None of her sons is happy in the field she forced him into; they combine their talents and kill her, returning once a year to the farm to commemorate her mistaken theory.

"The Iron Chancellor" (1958) deals with the Frankenstein theme in a much different mood. The Carmichael family purchases a new roboservitor, Bismarck, to act as their cook. He has built-in "reducing monitors" which can be programmed so that he will help them lose weight. They become his prisoners, virtually starving to death. Silverberg's attitude toward the American business community surfaces in his portrayal of the company's sales and maintenance representative, Robinson. He rescues the Carmichaels by turning Bismarck off, but he is so intrigued by the many mistakes in its circuitry which may somehow herald a "breakthrough in robotic science" that he inadvertently reactivates Bismarck, becoming one of its prisoners. So excited is he at the prospect of manufacturing "self-willed" robots that he can only exclaim, " . . . and think of what that means to science." [18] Like many other businessmen whom Silverberg was to create, Robinson forgot—or ignored—the consequences for mankind.

Consequences have remained a definite element governing Silverberg's speculations. In "New Men for Mars" (1957), for example, Brian Aherne must evalute the success of the Martian colony made up of a polyglot of intellectuals before the United Nations will renew its appropriation. He finds that the colony has prospered beneath its plastic dome. He finds, too, that Eschebara, who opposed the original plan for the colony, has peopled a second dome with native Peruvians conditioned to the high altitude of the Andes. He argues that they will adapt more quickly to the harsh Martian environment. Aherne decides to endorse the established colony and ignore Eschebara's efforts. Only after an earthquake has destroyed both domes does he realize that the two groups must intermarry so that a new race having both intelligence and the needed stamina will populate Mars. Yet in "Misfit" he champions the physical and psychological strengths of man, suggesting that these qualities are superior to those of a population which has been genetically engineered to live on a planet whose gravity is much heavier than Earth's. "Double Dare" (1956), in which Earthmen and the alien Domerangi exchange teams of engineers, also celebrates the inventiveness of man.

The protagonist of "Hidden Talent" (1957) also triumphs over his problem. Possessing extraordinary telekinetic powers, Rygor Davison is sent by the Esper Guild to the planet Mondarran IV and must remain there for five years while he learns to control his abilities. He must conceal them, for the society of Mondarran IV burns witches. To save himself, he becomes an itinerant magician.

In contrast, "The Four" (1958) focuses upon Mary Foyle, who a hundred years after an atomic holocaust uses her psi power to project herself beyond Undersea Refuge PL-12 (New Baltimore) to other such shelters. Because she alone cannot reach the surface, she unites her mind with those of three young men. Together they envision a pastoral landscape instead of radioactive desolation. Captured by authorities, the four are ejected into the sea. They gain the surface; as she dies of radiation poisoning, one of her companions tells her that he has tricked her into seeing a beautiful land. New Baltimore is also destroyed, for the sea engulfs it, crushing the gate which had been opened long enough to cast out the undesirables. In "World of a Thousand Colors" (1957), the protagonist fails a test; because he is a murderer, he cannot join himself with six others into a single being and so is killed. A simple story, it nevertheless anticipates the concern with isolation and transcendence which permeates the later fiction.

Yet Silverberg most often turns to the encounter between Earthman and alien to explore his themes. "Blaze of Glory" (1957) concentrates upon the irascible Murchison, a man who loves his privacy and refuses to do anything he does not want to do. On Shaula II he strikes a native who enters his cabin. During the ship's return to Earth, while it is in warp, something goes wrong with the ion-drive so that the instruments cannot establish the coordinates needed to land. Murchison volunteers to go outside and guide the ship by voice. He burns to a crisp as it enters the Earth's atmosphere. The narrator wonders whether or not the gentle Shaulans sabotaged the ship and somehow compelled Murchison to go to his death.

In retrospect, one can see in "Journey's End" (1958) something of the mood that colors the opening of *Downward to the Earth* (1970). Barchay goes to a V'leeg village after an absence of twenty years. His wife died long ago, and his son was killed within the past year during a brief insurrection of the aliens. Barchay feels completely alone until, as he is slain by the aliens, he realizes that he has left behind an illegitimate, half-V'leeg son whose mother he seduced when she was a mere girl and he last came to the village.

"Mind for Business" (1956) gives the encounter a lighter touch. The protagonist, Connolly, kidnaps the Chief of Staff of the Nidlans, who are planning a war with Earth. Caught in a booby-trap that forces him down on an isolated planet and wrecks his ship, Connolly sends out an SOS. Both the Nidlans and another alien race, the Corilano, send ships disguised as Terran merchant-men, but Connolly immediately fires on both. A third merchant-man rescues him as the captains of the alien ships wonder what error they made. They listen to a tape and hear Connolly and the captain of the real Earth ship haggle about who will pay for the cost of the rescue. Not only do the Nidlans reject the idea of war, they also hope that one day they will be as clever as the Earthmen.

But humor is rare. The satire aimed at the business community in "The Iron Chancellor" is directed at the military in "Ozymandias" (1958). On a world that has been dead for a million years—not even a blade of grass grows—the anthropologists among the crew find a robot that possesses all knowledge of the Thaiquens, even having read all of the books from the libraries of the long-vanished civilization. They try to keep their find a secret, for the expedition is financed primarily by the General Staff of the Armed Forces of the United States. The presence of the anthropologists is a mere gesture; the aim of the ship's commander, Colonel Mattern, is to obtain military information. He seizes the robot, explaining that it will provide the U.S. with undreamed-of weapons, thus making the nation invulnerable. Echoes of Shelley's poem sound throughout the narrative as the anthropologists realize that in the sands of the barren world lies the fate of Earth.

"The Overlord's Thumb" (1957) provides a sharp contrast, probably because its protagonist, Colonel John Devall, is an anthropologist before he is a military man. When one of his lieutenants unwittingly desecrates a shrine (a flowering bush) and kills an alien in self defense, Devall turns the officer over to the aliens for trial despite the protestations of his senior officers who assert that Earth will lose prestige by giving in to the natives. The lieutenant is acquitted, an old priest brings gifts, and Devall realizes, "For the first time, Earth had made a concrete demonstration of the equality-of-intelligent-life doctrine it had been preaching so long." [19]

In some ways, however, the most important of these early contact stories is "Certainty" (1959), whose protagonist, the commander of an Earth warship, would risk ending a century of galactic peace because an alien spaceship has landed on a planet claimed by Earth to carry out certain observations. He delivers an ultimatum, but first several of his officers and then he himself goes directly against his ultimatum by allowing the Halivanu to remain where they are until they complete their work. Its importance lies in the fact that it appears to be the first story in which Silverberg mentions the ability of an alien race whose psychic powers enable them to disrupt a man's mind, [20] a theme which was to shape so much of his fiction during the mid-1960's.

"Translation Error" (1959), one of his most frequently reprinted stories, combines the encounter with aliens and the time paradox theme. A seemingly benevolent race of aliens keeps watch over Earth. Karn, their representative, brought World War I to an end in 1916 through the Treaty of Dusseldorf. When he next visits the Earth, however, to his consternation he finds himself in a different time continuum amidst the cold war of the 1950's. He meets himself, of course, and his opposite berates his attempts to reduce mankind to "vegetables" unable to attain space flight. When he manages to return to his own continuum, he learns that although man has been deprived of his escalating technology, he has developed his psychic powers. The first ambassador from Earth had teleported to Hethivar five weeks earlier. A treaty of peace had been signed on Earth's terms.

In 'Mugwump Four'' (1959) Silverberg abandons the galactic stage. Al Miller finds himself shuttled from the present both forward in time to 2431 and back and forth between one continuum and another after he inadvertently becomes involved (by dialing a phone number) in a war between mankind and a race of mutants, which lasts until the twenty-fifth century. In one continuum humanity exterminates the mutants; in the other, the struggle continues. Each side thinks Miller a spy for the other. When he returns to 1959, he finds that he is apparently caught in an endless cycle because again he has dialed the same number and gotten the same answer.

Other stories could be cited to illustrate Silverberg's versatility. "To Be Continued" (1956) explores the longevity of 2000-year-old Gaius Titus Menenius, who learns from a medical report that (at last) he can become a father. Assuming the various identities which he maintains in the modern world, he searches for a wife and, luckily, finds a young woman who shares his longevity. During her first identity, however, she sailed as a passenger on the Mayflower so that, unfortunately, she is the equivalent of a three-year-old and cannot bear children for at least a thousand years. The narrator of "Eve and the Twenty-four Adams" (1957) is the Psych Officer of the warship *Donnybrook*; he tells how he recruited Eve Tyler as "crew girl" and took her to the Sirian war zone, where he learned that she was to be his daughter-in-law. Because she would not cooperate with the men, he drugged her; she remembers nothing of her sexual experiences. In "Prime Commandment" (1957) the descendants of the survivors of a wrecked generation ship have reverted to a primitive culture, but they have built their religion around a mixture of the accident and their memories of Christianity. A second ship, carrying members of the Church of the New Resurrection, arrives on the planet. That evangelical congregation expects, of course, to convert what they regard as naked savages, but they themselves are massacred because they rest on the Sabbath and because the natives will have no other god before their ship. When one recalls *Tower of Glass* (1970), the most intriguing aspect of this story is the litany the natives have developed around their memories of the ship's history.

Of all of the short stories from the period, "Passport to Sirius" (1958) perhaps best exemplifies Silverberg's criticism of the American establishment. Its protagonist, Consumer Sixth Class David Carman, learns that the government has deliberately saturated the news media with false accounts of warfare with Sirius IV to control fluctuations of the economy (" . . . spending increases in direct proportion to adverse military news" [21]). When he returns from Sirius IV with photographic evidence that there has never been a war, he is informed that the government ended that war. A new conflict will soon begin in the sector of the Great Andromeda Nebula—a distance that he cannot travel. The story's similarity to *Invaders from Earth* needs no comment.

Perhaps this selection of stories and novels from the late 1950's will adequately indicate that there never was a discontinuity in the science fiction Silverberg wrote. From the beginning, he was a skilled storyteller. Throughout the fiction are themes and plot-lines that he would develop in his later fiction. What was essential was that he gain independence so that he would not have to live on his science-fiction output.

NOTES

1. Robert Silverberg, "Sounding Brass, Tinkling Cymbal," in *Hell's Cartographers*, eds. Brian W. Aldiss and Harry Harrison (London: Weidenfeld and Nicolson, 1975), p. 11.
2. Silverberg, p. 13.
3. Floyd C. Gale, *Galaxy*, 13 (May 1956), 103; P. Schuyler Miller, *Astounding*, 55 (June 1956), 147; Hans Stefan Santesson, *Fantastic Universe*, 5 (April 1956), 128.
4. Silverberg, "Introduction," *Science Fiction Greats*, No. 13 (Winter 1969), inside front cover.
5. Silverberg, "Sounding Brass, Tinkling Cymbal," pp. 20, 22.
6. Anthony Boucher, *F&SF*, 13 (August 1957), 108; 13 (November 1957), 118.
7. Thomas D. Clareson, "Robert Silverberg: The Compleat Writer," *F&SF*, 46 (April 1974), 75.
8. P. Schuyler Miller, *Analog*, 64 (December 1959), 148-149.
9. Miller, *Analog*, 64 (November 1959), 150-151.
10. Silverberg, "Introduction," *Stepsons of Terra* (New York: Ace Books, 1977), p. xi.
11. Anon., *Kirkus Reviews*, 33 (1 September 1965), 914; Peter J. Henniken-Heaton, *Christian Science Monitor*, 57 (4 November 1965), B8.

12. Silverberg, "Introduction," *Stepsons of Terra*, p. x.
13. Silverberg, "Sounding Brass, Tinkling Cymbal," p. 28.
14. Silverberg, "En Route to Earth," *Dimension Thirteen* (New York: Ballantine Books, 1969), p. 132.
15. Silverberg, "Sounding Brass, Tinkling Cymbal," p. 22.
16. Silverberg, untitled headline to "Road to Nightfall," *The Best of Robert Silverberg* (New York: Pocket Books, 1976), p. 1.
17. Clareson, "The Fictions of Robert Silverberg," in *Voices for the Future*, ed. Thomas D. Clareson (Bowling Green, Ohio: Bowling Green Popular Press, 1979), II, 6.
18. Silverberg, "The Iron Chancellor," *Needle in a Timestack* (New York: Ballantine Books, 1966), p. 189.
19. Silverberg, "The Overlord's Thumb," *Invaders from Earth* and *To Worlds Beyond* (New York: Ace Books, 1980), p. 323.
20. Silverberg, "Certainty," *Invaders from Earth* and *To Other Worlds*, p. 351.
21. Silverberg, "Passport to Sirius," *Needle in a Timestack*, p. 33.

II

TRANSITION: 1960 - 1967

As noted, the second part of the myth of Robert Silverberg turns on the idea that after 1959 he broke all ties with science fiction and, for a number of years at least, returned only occasionally to the field, beginning especially in *Galaxy*, where at the invitation of Frederik Pohl he began to publish those quality stories leading to those works on which his reputation of the 1970's must rest. As so often with legend, this is no more than a half truth. Ironically, one of the last novels which he wrote in 1959—a juvenile—was published in 1960 as *Lost Race of Mars*. *The New York Times* named it one of the hundred best children's books of the year, the highest recognition any of his work had received by that date.

In "Sounding Brass, Tinkling Cymbal," Silverberg himself provides the key to what happened during the transitional early 1960's. After a trip to Pompeii, he suggested a non-fiction book aimed at the juvenile audience and based upon the archaeological excavations at the Roman site. Through the influence of his agent, Henry Morrison, he expanded the idea to include a number of ruins—among them Chichen Itza, Angkor, and Babylon—in *Lost Cities and Vanished Civilizations*. In April, 1962, G. P. Putnam's Sons published it. It was named one of the five best books of the year for the juvenile audience, and the Junior Literary Guild chose it as one of its selections.

By the time of its publication, Silverberg had discovered that he "had more work than I could handle in the lucrative juvenile non-fiction hardcover field." [1] But that in itself is not the whole story, for without interruption from 1960 onward he turned out a wide variety of books at the same compulsive rate of production that he had maintained earlier while writing science fiction. Between *Treasures Beneath the Sea* (1960) and *The World within the Tide Pool* (1972), using a number of pseudonyms—chief among them Walker Chapman and Lee Sebastien—he wrote some seventy books, to say nothing of a variety of factual articles for periodicals ranging from *High Fidelity* and *Amazing Stories* (a series entitled "Scientific Hoaxes," which formed the core of a book) to *Natural History*, *Today's Health*, and *Saturday Review*. He became a popularizer of science, drawing primarily upon his long-standing interests in prehistory, archaeology, and exploration, although under pseudonyms he also took on assignments in history, politics, and labor relations.

From 1960 through 1965, although his records may not be complete, he collaborated on at least seven novels for which he received no public acknowledgment. This figure ignores the fact that during these same years he produced the majority of his one hundred or more soft-pornography titles as Don Elliot/Eliot. He has acknowledged that during the first half of the 1960's, at least, he continued to write well over a million words a year. In addition, in 1966 he edited his first anthology, *Earthmen and Strangers*. By 1981 he had issued sixty-seven anthologies, the most famous of which was the *New Directions* series, for which he was several times nominated for the Hugo award as the best professional editor of the year.

The importance of all of this to his subsequent development after 1960 as one of the leading, innovative science-fiction writers rests basically on two often overlooked facts. First, as he himself has said, "For the first time since I became a professional writer, nearly a decade earlier, I won my own respect," [2] primarily for his work in juvenile non-fiction. Perhaps even more important, through this varied market he gained financial independence without having to grind out science-fiction potboilers. The cost, however, remained high, for he continued his high rate of productivity, a factor which undoubtedly contributed to his illness of 1966.

But the idea that he cut himself off completely from the field of science fiction, however briefly, is completely erroneous. To begin with, his earliest collections of short stories appeared: *Next Stop the Stars* (1962); *Godling, Go Home* (1964); *To Worlds Beyond* (1965); and *Needle in a Timestack* (1966). Only the last of these volumes contained stories originally written and published in the 1960's; otherwise, they drew their selections entirely from the years 1955 through 1959. As previously noted, there were the novellas and a single serial from that same period which did not see book publication until after 1960: *Collision Course* (1961), *Recalled to Life* (1962), *The Silent Invaders* (1963), *Conquerors from the Darkness* (1965), and finally, *Three Survived* (1969). One cannot be certain when these works were revised and expanded into book-length narratives; nor can one be sure when Silverberg wrote *One of Our Asteroids Is Missing* (1964), issued under the name of Calvin M. Knox, the last time that he used a pseudonym with a novel.

The Seed of Earth typifies the problem of dating any of his longer work issued during the early 1960's. He has explained that he originally wrote it in the autumn of 1958, building it from "The Winds of Siros" (1957), which he incorporated into the narrative beginning with chapter eleven. [3] But not until after two rejections and an unexpected editorial delay did it appear simultaneously in June, 1962, as a novella in *Galaxy* and as an Ace paperback—though the texts differed. It has a special importance because it is the first of his novels to give extensive attention to psychic cannibalism, a motif basic to the so-called dark side of his fiction.

Without explicit information from Silverberg, particularly since there have been no subsequent editions of either novel as yet, one can only wonder when he wrote both *Planet of Death* (1967), which was panned critically, and *Those Who Watch* (1967), which apparently received no reviews at all. [4] That neglect reflects more upon the critics than upon the quality of the short novel. In *Those Who Watch* Silverberg dealt with a favorite theme in a new manner. For thousands of years two alien races—the Dirnan and the Krazanoi—have kept Earth under surveillance, but they have done so peacefully, remaining "aloof" from terrestrial affairs. Instead of a far-distant future, Silverberg draws upon the popular interest in flying saucers and projects only to 1982. Rather than developing a complex plot, he concentrates upon what happens to the three Dirnans who abandon their ship just before it explodes over northern New Mexico, an accident seen from Taos and Santa Fe to Albuquerque. Each is injured upon landing. Although the Krazanoi, other Dirnans, and members of the Atmospheric Objects Survey team hunt for the survivors, Silverberg keeps such action to a minimum. His interest lies with the relationships each member of the crew has with a human (the Dirnans have been "built" so that outwardly they appear to be human). Significantly, two of the relationships are sexual. Vorneen and Kathryn Mason, conveniently a former nurse whose husband was killed a year earlier, parallel Glair and Colonel Tom Falkner, an alcoholic who was washed out of the Astronaut program and became a member of AOS. At the end of the novel, after they have been separated from their alien lovers, Kathryn and Tom seem a potential couple. The most interesting relationship, however, is that between the eldest of the Dirnans, Mirtin, and Charley Estancia, a young boy who belongs to the San Miguel Pueblo. Charley is intellectually awakened, dreaming of becoming a spaceman. *Those Who Watch* must be judged as an important transitional novel, primarily for its emphasis upon characterization and its realistic portrayal of the near-future. A minor but intriguing element is the "Contact Cult," a new religion based upon the concept of man's frequent contact with superhuman galactic beings, an idea toward which Silverberg is coldly hostile.

25

Amid so much fiction one can easily forget that from April, 1964, through August, 1965, Silverberg conducted the review column, "The Spectroscope" for *Amazing Stories* and "Fantasy Books" for *Fantastic* in the winter and spring of 1965. Previously, in 1958 and 1959, under the pseudonym of Calvin M. Knox, he had written "Readin' and Writin'" for *SFA*, while doing a few columns of *"Infinity's Choice"* under his own name. In a sense this five-year lapse from reviewing constitutes Silverberg's major absence from the field of science fiction, for as has been shown, even without considering the stories intended specifically for *Galaxy*, he published fiction throughout the period.

Yet during the first half of the decade, the majority of his new books—at least a dozen—were aimed at the juvenile non-fiction market. Despite the success of *Lost Race of Mars* (1960), he did not produce another novel for the juvenile audience until *Regan's Planet* (1964), a tale focusing upon the tribulations of a young protagonist who stages a World's Fair celebrating the five-hundredth anniversary of Columbus' discovery of America. P. Schuyler Miller did not think Silverberg adequately developed the "wonderful idea" implicit in the story, but Judith Merril used the occasion—one of her few reviews of Silverberg—to assert that "with respect to them both, [he can] be compared to Murray Leinster for honest craftsmanship." [5] Similarly, *Time of the Great Freeze* (1964) gained mixed reactions, although many reviewers found it an "exciting" adventure story. Centuries after a new ice age has frozen the Atlantic and destroyed modern civilization, the youthful Jim Barnes, his father, and several companions leave subterranean New York to trek across the ice to re-establish communication with London. A straightforward narrative, it is memorable chiefly for the episodes involving the primitive peoples whom the expedition encounters.

Although *The Mask of Akhnaten* (1965) is the only one of his novels that cannot be classified as science fiction (in an "Author's Note," he refers to it as "a mixture of fact and fantasy" [6]), it does make use of his knowledge of archaeology, particularly information he had included in *Empires in the Dust* (1963) and *Akhnaten: the Rebel Pharaoh* (1964). Its storyline takes the fifteen-year-old Tom Lloyd and his journalist uncle into the Upper Nile Valley before the completion of the Aswan Dam; there they discover the lost tomb of Akhnaten.

In contrast to this "real-life adventure," as its dustjacket calls it, *The Gate of Worlds* (1967) achieves its effectiveness largely because of the appeal of the imaginary society Silverberg creates, drawing once again upon his interests in archaeology and history. *The Gate of Worlds* is his only juvenile portraying an alternate world. It takes as its point of departure the premise that the Black Death of the fourteenth century killed three-quarters of the population of Europe so that the Turks conquered the West, including England, while the militant Aztecs dominated Mexico and parts of North America (the Upper Hesperides), although there remained the constant threat of warfare between them and the Incan empire. The American continents had been discovered by accident in 1585 when a Portugese ship commanded by Diogo Lobo was blown across the "Ocean Sea" from Africa. The Aztec king, Moctezuma III, executed at least some of the sailors, with the result that as late as the time of the story—1963—there had been no European colonization of the Americas, although the Russians had established at least one "town" on the western coast beyond the reach of Aztec influence. This framework gives Silverberg a unique perspective from which to criticize American and, especially, European imperialism.

The first-person, episodic narrative—presented as a memoir—allows Dan Beauchamp of London (New Istanbul) to travel from Aztec Mexico to the barren Southwest, the Pacific coast, and even the Mississippi valley. He falls in love with the daughter of an Indian chief, the beautiful Takinaktu, who has been corrupted by the Russians; they have taught her Turkish because she wished to read Shakespeare "in his original language" (besides *Julius Caesar*, *Macbeth*, and *Hamlet*, he had written *Suleiman the Magnificent* and *Osman the Great*). The open-ending makes the reader hope for a sequel: after quarreling with Takinaktu and becoming separated from her, Dan attempts to follow her to Africa, "the coming place, the next dominant continent." [7]

The quality of *The Gate of Worlds* is surpassed only by Silverberg's finest juvenile, *Across a Billion Years* (1969). Whereas the former shares much of the literary texture of the best fiction Silverberg was writing by 1967, the latter also presents a number of the themes important to his mature novels. Published in the same year that saw the serialization of *Downward to the Earth* begin, *Across a Billion Years* is also structured as a quest. Its first-person narrator, Tom Rice, joins a group of archaeologists searching for artifacts of the Mirt Korp Ahm, an ancient race, "the so-called High Ones, whose civilization once spread throughout the galaxy." [8] An incidental scene, in which Rice talks with the beautiful android woman, Kelly, anticipates one of the central concerns of *Tower of Glass* (1970). To Rice's assertion that creating "life in a laboratory vat is . . . godlike," Kelly retorts, "And so . . . you godlike ones show your godlike natures by feeling superior to the artificial human beings you create. . . . Why not simply accept all the distinctions and concentrate on matters of real importance." [9]

When the quest leads the group to the home world of the Mirt Korp Ahm, they discover a "thought amplifier," which Rice considers a gift from that ancient race. It can benefit not only mankind but "*all* organic life-forms." Initially, Rice uses it to unite himself with the telepathic minority which serves as a galactic communications network and then with one of his companions: " . . . our minds met and became one." The experience leads him to speculate that "it is an end to secrecy and suspicion, of misunderstanding, of quarrels, of isolation, of flawed communications, of separation." [10] These are aspects of the human condition which increasingly obsessed the protagonists of Silverberg's fiction during the 1960's and 1970's. That concern for them appears in *Across a Billion Years* and indicates, obviously, that he was working on it during the same period in which he was writing the novels intended for an adult audience. Although a sense of affirmation seems stronger in *Across a Billion Years*, he did not simplify the outcome because he was addressing a juvenile audience. He allowed Rice to speculate that " . . . we're going to make plenty of mistakes before we know how to handle these powers . . ." [11] There is hope for unity and understanding, but the statement that dominates one's final impression of the novel occurs when Rice takes off the thought amplifier, thereby ending his telepathic union. He laments, "I was alone, terribly alone, once more locked into my skull." [12] This individual isolation—the image of man as a prisoner within his own mind—vividly underscores what may be the core of Silverberg's continuing concerns. Based largely upon the failure of communication and understanding, it points to those problems that shaped the pessimistic mood of so much of his fiction during the 1960's and 1970's.

NOTES

1. Silverberg, "Sounding Brass, Tinkling Cymbal," p. 28.
2. Silverberg, "Sounding Brass, Tinkling Cymbal," p. 28.
3. Silverberg, "Introduction," *The Seed of Earth* (New York: Ace Books, 1977), pp. xii-xiv.
4. H. W. Hall, *Science Fiction Book Review Index 1923-1973* (Detroit: Gale Research Company, 1975), pp. 281-282. Hall lists no reviews of either *Planet of Death* or *Those Who Watch*. However, at least two reviews of *Planet of Death* do exist: Ruth Roth, *Library Journal*, 92 (November 15, 1967), 4257-4258; and Robert Cohen, *Young Readers Review* 4 (November 1967), 6.
5. P. Schuyler Miller, *Analog*, 74 (November 1964), 89; Judith Merril, *F&SF*, 28 (March 1965), 57.
6. Silverberg, *The Mask of Akhnaten* (New York: The Macmillan Company, 1965), p. 181.
7. Silverberg, *The Gate of Worlds* (New York: Holt, Rinehart and Winston, 1967), p. 198.
8. Clareson, "Silverberg: The Compleat Writer," *F&SF*, 46

(April 1974), 77.

9. Silverberg, *Across a Billion Years* (New York: Dial Press, 1969), pp. 145-146, as cited by Clareson, "Silverberg: The Compleat Writer," 77.

10. Silverberg, *Across a Billion Years*, p. 247, as cited by Clareson, p. 77.

11. Silverberg, *Across a Billion Years*, p. 249, as cited by Clareson, p. 78.

12. Silverberg, *Across a Billion Years*, p. 246, as cited by Clareson, "The Fictions of Robert Silverberg," p. 16.

III

THE DARK SIDE OF SILVERBERG'S FICTION
1957 - 1968

When writers and critics have referred to science fiction as a stereotypical, formulaic fiction, they have had in mind definite patterns which shaped science fiction especially in the mass market, pulp magazines as early as Munsey's *All Story* and *Argosy*. From these early periodicals, the so-called specialist magazines—like *Amazing Stories*, *Astounding Stories*, *Weird Tales*, and even such "hero-pulps" as *Doc Savage*, *G-8 and His Battle Aces*, and *Operator #5*—inherited certain conventions in terms of narrative technique, plot, and theme which they simply crystallized because their mass market, supposedly made up chiefly of young males, liked such stories. Essentially, despite a frequent reliance upon the first-person point of view to gain credibility, early science fiction concerned itself with external action rather than character study. It became one kind of adventure story. One may argue that each editor emphasized favorite conventions, thereby giving individual identity to, at least, the best of the science-fiction titles. For example, John W. Campbell's *Astounding* seemed to favor the theme of man's scientific achievements that permitted him to spread throughout the galaxies. One is hard pressed to think of a story in *Astounding/ Analog*, especially before 1970, in which aliens truly bested mankind, whatever the endeavor or conflict. One may also argue that the controversy during the late 1960's centering around the "new wave" was nothing more nor less than the climax of a deliberate effort by various writers to escape the established patterns through introducing techniques and materials new to the field, although they may have long been a part of the dominant current of nineteenth- and twentieth-century realism.

At the Modern Language Association Forum on Science Fiction in 1968, this effort led Lester del Rey to assert that "science fiction is the myth-making principal of human nature today." Although previous myths in western society had looked backward toward both a golden age and demons, now "science, knowledge, experience have largely destroyed those myths. The new wave in sf is crying that without these myths man is a degraded and indecent animal, doomed to failure against the utter evils of the cosmos, That is the new wave as it was really meant originally. It is, in other words, naturalism transferred to sf, where it doesn't fit very well.'' [1] At the same meeting Silverberg reprimanded the panel for speaking of the predictive nature of science fiction without considering the "images and visions and dreams" which writers were aiming at; in other words, for not discussing "science fiction as literature.'' [2] He referred to the earlier stages of this change in the field when he wrote in "Sounding Brass, Tinkling Cymbal" of the "old pulp-magazine rigidities" dissolving and of "an army of younger, or at any rate newer writers . . . boldly overturn[ing] the traditional rules" during the period 1962-1965 when he began to contribute occasional stories to *Galaxy*. [3]

Usually, a science-fiction story had been told in a straightforward manner—beginning, middle, and end—because it had dealt with an heroic figure who overcame all obstacles, be they terrestrial monsters, mad scientists, or tentacled aliens. One of the most obviously rigid forms has descended through Edgar Rice Burroughs and Robert E. Howard—the sword-and-sorcery motif, which seldom varies whether or not the protagonist is male or female. One consequence of such patterning has been the domination of the problem—or puzzle—story which has led to the comparison of science fiction and detective fiction. As a result, on the one hand, one may speak of the tradition of the Enlightenment within science fiction; on the other, of Romanticism. [4]

Yet what authors and critics alike have too often forgotten is that individual writers, like Silverberg, have attempted throughout their careers to make innovations, both technically and thematically. The best of science fiction has never remained a static form. Similarly, Silverberg's work does not exhibit a simplistic, linear development. From the outset, as noted, he produced the occasional quality story which did not readily sell. Before he began to experiment consciously with narrative technique and style, in "Warm Man" (1957) he made an initial exploration of the theme with which he so often dramatized his increasing pessimism and despair.

In it, he chose to work "with realistic characters in a contemporary setting instead of with spacefarers and alien creatures.'' [5] He introduces Mr. Hallinan, a strangely solitary man who nevertheless ingratiates himself into suburban New Brewster because he is willing to listen attentively to his companions who compulsively unburden themselves to him. He thus becomes essential to many of his emotionally crippled neighbors, particularly the women; they feel that he alone understands them. He soaks up their troubles "*like a sponge*,'' but after such sessions he spends a day at home as though "he's going to digest" the confessions of

31

frustration and inadequacy which have been fed him. Abruptly, spearheaded by the reaction of some of the men, the community comes to distrust him—to exclude him—having grown "weary, perhaps, of his constant empathy for their woes." [6] Alone again, he comes upon nine-year-old Lonny Dewitt, who is being harassed by his companions, and asks the boy to tell what is bothering him; " . . . years of repression and torment came rolling out in one roaring burst." [7] The telepathic Lonny—a sender—overwhelms Mr. Hallinan—a receiver—killing him. As he dies, Hallinan realizes bitterly, "I . . . was . . . a . . . leach."

In the same year the potential of "Warm Man" assumed its most enduring form in "The Winds of Siros," which, as noted, provided the climactic action of *The Seed of Earth* (1962). Into this tale of one of Earth's attempts to colonize a distant planet, Silverberg introduces "a study of human psychosexual interactions"; to accomplish this, he makes use of what he has acknowledged as one of "my later themes and obsessions . . . the aliens who place human beings in a condition of stress for hidden purposes of their own." [8] Immediately upon the colonists' arrival on the planet, the men are forced to choose wives without really knowing any of the women. The first night aliens seize two of the new couples and carry them to a cave. Daily they feed the humans; otherwise, they simply gather on the plain nearby. During the next five days, the relationships among the humans deteriorate, running the gamut of emotions. The protagonist, Mike Dawes, wonders if the aliens "enjoyed the performance"; then, realizes that the "ugly ape-things . . . grabbed us out of the colony and stuck us up here so they could listen in on our emotions, soak them up, feed on them . . . . They knew damned well what would happen. They knew we'd start hating each other, that we'd fight and quarrel and build walls around ourselves. That's what they wanted us to do. It would be a sort of circus for them—a purge, maybe. A kind of entertainment." [9] Knowing this, the four cooperate. Although animosities have brought about a switching of partners, the four build a rope ladder and return to the colony unmolested by the obviously telepathic aliens.

The theme of isolation became the central issue of "To See the Invisible Man" (1962), the first work which he submitted to Frederik Pohl for publication in *Galaxy*. From Silverberg's comments, he seems to date his return to science fiction as a serious artist from that story, which he developed from an incidental line in Jorge Luis Borges' "The Babylon Lottery." [10] Silverberg's first-person narrator explains that because of his unwillingness to reveal his innermost feelings and problems to members of his society—the sin of "coldness"—he is officially punished after a trial by being completely ignored by that society for a year. The narrative chronicles the unnamed protagonist's loneliness and despair. Although he is instantly welcomed back after the end of his punishment, he rejects the society when he embraces another individual who has been condemned to social invisibility.

The condemnation of society continued in "The Pain Peddlers" (1963), a brief glimpse of the extent to which television will do anything to feed its audience's apparently insatiable appetite for vicarious pain. The use of an "EEG-amplifer" allows viewers to share the brain waves of those in pain.

At the heart of Silverberg's anguish and pessimism, however, lies "Flies" (1967), which he wrote specifically for Harlan Ellison's anthology, *Dangerous Visions*. Commenting on it almost a decade later, he explained that its "theme touched on psychic cannibalism [his first use of that expression]—its main character would be a man who feeds on the emotional distress of others—and the story was built on the bleak view of the universe as a place in which huge, impersonal forces, acting without motives comprehensible to human beings, affect our lives in seemingly random ways." [11] In the same passage he called *Thorns* (1967) "a second version" of the short story and further acknowledged its centrality by pointing out that such novels as *The Man in the Maze* (1968) and the controversial *Dying Inside* (1972) echo its theme and plot.

Its point of departure is the gratuitous act of the surgeons of an alien race—"the golden ones"; they restore a dead starman, Cassiday, to life by "repairing" him from a few pieces left after the implosion of his ship. In doing so, they provide him with a greater sensitivity, including "new hungers . . . certain abilities." [12] They permit him to return to Earth so that he can act as a kind of transmitter, sending them the emotions of anyone whom he encounters. One infers that mere curiosity governs the aliens' actions. In some unexplained way, Cassiday has become less than human; at one point he remarks, "I'm a god now, did you know that?" [13] Incapable of emotion, he destroys his former wives. He gives drugs to Beryl, who had broken the habit; he strangles the devoted Ganymedean pet of Mirabel, who is desperately lonely; he kicks pregnant Laureen, who loses her baby. Only then, appalled, do the golden ones bring Cassiday back to their world to adjust him. They restore his conscience, but they also turn his perceptions inward so that he must "feed on his own misery like a vulture tearing out its entrails." Then they let him go: "*nailed to his cross*." [14]

Among his short stories only "Passengers" (1968), which gained him his first Nebula Award, surpasses "Flies" in its dark vision of the universe. For three years human beings have served as hosts for parasitic aliens—the Passengers who ride them. The first-person narrator, who has just been released, believes that he has been "permitted" to recognize the young woman with whom he slept while she, too, was possessed. Desperately he attempts to establish a human relationship with her; just as it appears that he may succeed, another Passenger seizes him, forcing him into a homosexual liaison. The protagonist speaks of the human situation in terms of "the old problem, free will versus determinism, translated into the foulest of forms. Determinism is no longer a philosopher's abstraction; it is cold alien tendrils sliding between the cranial sutures." [15] He asks if the sense of freedom is ever more than a illusion. This is a theme which Silverberg will most fully explore in *The Stochastic Man* (1975). He has remembered the short story primarily because it was the first which he wrote entirely in the present tense, a mode which "has become an easily recognizable stylistic mannerism" of his. [16]

One looks for reasons which explain why Silverberg's pessimism reached a high point during the mid and late 1960's. Not all of his fiction shared his bleakest mood, although most of it, implicitly at least, reveals his growing dissatisfaction with the potential of American society and politics. From the early story, "Hopper" (1956), he developed the novel, *The Time Hoppers* (1967), whose protagonist, Quellen, as noted, escapes from an over-populated future world to pre-Columbian America. *Hawksbill Station*, first as a novella in *Galaxy* (1967) and then as a novel (1968), combines Silverberg's interests in prehistory and time travel. In the twenty-first century, society casts its political undesirables back into the later Cambrian period (since America was "a continental slab of rock" during this period, without even grass or trees, to say nothing of major life-forms, the presence of the men could not change the future). The process was irreversible, although the society did supply a minimum of such supplies as building material. The novelization provides a somewhat fuller picture of the society "up front," but the narrative's focus remains with Barrett, "the uncrowned king of Hawksbill Station," who is both crippled and resigned to his exile. When a process is developed so that the prisoners can be returned to their own time, Barrett volunteers to stay behind to keep the Station running and to advise the scientists who will be coming back. Again the central image is that of a solitary man, one who rejects society and survives in a barren world. *Hawksbill Station* was the first of Silverberg's works to gain nominations for the Nebula and the Hugo, although it did not win either.

Despite the fact that neither *The Time Hoppers* nor *Hawksbill Station* has a conventionally "happy" ending, one wonders whether or not working with the concept of time travel somehow eased the tensions so apparent in much of Silverberg's other fiction. This surmise is strengthened by the fact that somewhat later when he was battling with other complex themes, he took time out to write *Up the Line* (1969), a ribald tale of the misadventures of a time courier who guides sightseers to various periods of the Byzantine Empire. Silverberg makes use of all the time paradoxes. The protagonist traps himself when he falls in love with his many-times great grandmother. Although it was also nominated for both the Nebula and Hugo awards, it received mixed reaction, especially from those reviewers in fandom who thought they should object to its delightfully bawdy sexuality.

In the search for the causes of his pessimism, one turns to Silverberg's autobiographical writing, although he has always been more willing to discuss his writing and public career than private matters. (This characteristic holds true, for the most part, in conversations with him as well. He is an essentially private person.) Yet he has explained that in June, 1966, he fell ill. "The symptoms answered well to leukemia and other dire things, but turned out to be only a metabolic change, a sudden hyperactivity of the thyroid gland. Such thyroid outbreaks, I learned, are often caused by the stress of prolonged overwork . . . ." Although he blamed the illness on the "forced marches of El Dorado"—a reference to *The Golden Dream* (1967), which he had been working on through much of 1966—one can suggest that this period of "prolonged overwork" had lasted since the mid-1950's. Not only did he produce more than a million words in 1956, 1960, and 1961, but as late as 1965 his output totaled more than a million-and-a-half words. He regained his health by the end of 1966, but one senses that the experience frightened him; it was a "startling event" to him, his first serious illness as an adult. He did not, however, immediately ease up his pace, for he completed the El Dorado book during the summer; began planning a book on the Mound Builders (*Mound Builders of Ancient America: the Archaeology of a Myth*, 1968, which was very well received and became "a standard reference item" [18]); and after Worldcon in Cleveland began the novel *Thorns*. He has insisted that by the end of the year he began to withdraw from his "lunatic work schedule"; in 1966 he "barely exceeded a million" words and has never again "been anywhere near that insane level of productivity . . . ." [19] Yet discounting his anthologies and collections of his own stories—which do require energy—in the space of three years between 1967 and 1970, he produced thirty-six books. "I was, in truth," he has written, "riding an incredible wave of creative energy. Perhaps it was overcompensation for my period of fatigue and illness in 1966, perhaps just a sense of liberation and excitement that came from knowing I was at last writing only what I wanted to write, as well as I could do it." [20] His pace continued unabated.

A second event occurred which had a more obvious effect on Silverberg. In 1962 he and Barbara had purchased the Fiorello LaGuardia mansion; in the winter of 1968 fire destroyed Silverberg's third floor office/study, including many of his books and papers. The couple was driven out into the night; nine months were required to repair the damage to the house. In "Sounding Brass, Tinkling Cymbal," as well as personal conversations, he has captured something of the lasting effect of the tragedy. "But I was never the same again. Until the night of the fire I had never, except perhaps at the onset of my illness in 1966, been touched by the real anguish of life . . . . But now I had literally passed through the flames. The fire and more personal upheavals some months earlier had marked an end to my apparent immunity to life's pain, and drained from me, evidently forever, much of the bizarre energy that had allowed me to write a dozen or more books of high quality in a single year." The creative process became more laborious; gone was the "dynamic sense of clear vision that enabled me to write even the most taxing of my books in wild joyous spurts." Increasingly, he found that he had to do numerous drafts before he could "type final copy." [21]

If one combines the effects of the lengthy period of time during which Silverberg pressured himself to turn out his works—"joyous spurts," or not—with the traumatic effect of the flames of a winter's night, one has adequate substance, without inquiring into those other "upheavals," to understand something, at least, of the reasons for his subsequent concerns in his fiction. Yet these factors do not explain the original causes of his pessimism, for those stories and novels which mark the nadir of his dark vision were published by the end of 1968 and therefore had been completed by the time of the fire and its aftermath. As a result, one infers that these experiences confirmed a pessimism which Silverberg had previously arrived at intellectually for whatever reasons; their actual effect upon his writing showed itself as early as such novels as *Nightwings* (1969) and *Downward to the Earth* (1970) and as late as *The Stochastic Man* (1975) and *Shadrach in the Furnace* (1976) when he sought to find some resolution to his heightened sense of "the real anguish of life." Fom 1968 onward, his fiction expresses an emotional intensity largely absent from his earlier work.

Evidence supporting this interpretation may be found in both *Thorns* (1967) and *The Man in the Maze* (1968), the two novels which give perhaps the most unrelieved expression to his pessimism. Although the reader cannot escape the sense of despair felt by the respective protagonists, Minner Burris and Richard Muller, there remains about the novels a kind of cold detachment, rising in part from the objectivity of their narrative points of view, which makes them seem intellectual exercises in the study of human agony. The sado-masochism of Duncan Chalk provides the point of departure for *Thorns*. "In a large and indifferent universe" he stages "emotional feasts" for a "world [which] still took its pleasure in pain." Because Chalk is a "pain-responsive, pain-fed eater of emotion, depending on his intake of raw anguish as others did on their intake of bread and meat," he himself is also "the ultimate representative of his audience's tastes and so was perfectly able to supply that vast audience's inner needs." [22]

Always in search of sensations and surrounded by freaks, he decides not only to feed upon the relationship between a man and a woman but to share that experience with his audience. For the man he chooses the spaceman, Minner Burris, who has been operated on by alien surgeons who were apparently solely interested in the "secrets of human construction." [23] An aberration—in addition to internal changes, the aliens gave him tentacles and a strange skin—Burris exists in constant pain, isolating himself in his room. For the woman, Chalk selects Lona Kelvin, the chance subject of an experiment; human scientists took from her a hundred immature eggs which were hatched from bottles in six months. She was not allowed to carry one of her own babies. Chalk lures Burris by promising corrective surgery; he persuades Lona by suggesting that she may raise two of her children. Of this projected union, he remarks, "We'll try an experiment. Synergy. Catalysis. Bring them together. Who knows? We might generate some pain. Some human feeling . . . . We can learn lessons from pain. It teaches us that we're alive." [24]

Burris and Lona quarrel; torment one another; they separate. Chalk feasts on them. Not until they understand that he realized that they would loathe each other and only after they agree that there can be "no more hatred," do they turn upon Chalk, overwhelming him with their shared emotion—sympathy, if not love—"and kill him in a passage in which Silverberg evokes the images of Melville's White Whale and Marlowe's Faustus." [25] Because they also know that they cannot defeat a world which regards them as freaks, they return to the planet where Burris was operated on. As they depart, in a passage paralleling Chalk's earlier remarks, Burris explains to Lona: "To be alive—to feel, even to feel pain—how important that is . . . . Pain is instructive." [26]

Earlier, when Burris tells Lona why he has participated in Chalk's experiment and emerged from his seclusion, he asserts, "As a penance. As a deliberately chosen atonement for my withdrawal from the world. For the sake of discipline." [27] This reflection anticipates the role of two motifs that became ever more important to Silverberg's fiction as the 1960's drew to a close. Indeed, one may suggest that in his major novels the basic thematic struggle arises from the clash between a despairing pessimism and the hope of rising above the human condition through atonement and redemption. Although *Thorns* achieves no satisfactory resolution, one may consider it Silverberg's "fullest exploration of the redemptive power of pain in a natural world—an existential world outside the Christian tradition." [28]

Richard Muller, the protagonist of *The Man in the Maze*, also has fled from Earth. He once acted alone as the emissary to the Hydrans, the first race of aliens discovered. Although he thought they acted indifferently toward him and that no communication took place, when he returns to Earth, he learns that they somehow operated on him so that he cannot suppress his emotions. From him comes "this gush of self: a torrent of raw despair, a river of regrets and sorrow, all the sewage of the soil. He could not hold it back." [29] The aura was so strong that it drove away his sweetheart. He has isolated himself on a planet far from Earth in the ruins of an ancient city, the so-called maze of Lemnos. After Earthmen encounter another race of aliens—"colossal, unimaginable beasts . . . superwhales . . . forging a captive society" in which men "make outstanding slaves" [30]—an expedition comes to Lemnos to persuade him to act once more as mankind's emissary. At its simplest level, the storyline provides an example of science fiction as a puzzle in that initially robots and then men try to solve the booby-trapped maze, but that action merely provides a background for Muller's personal lamentations and for his dialogues with young Rawlins, who has been selected to lure him out of the ruins. Although Muller rages at himself both for the sin of pride in going alone among the Hydrans—instead of leading a team—and for the belief that he was somehow their mutilated god, Rawlins says of him, " . . . Muller's sorrows were not unique to himself; what he offered was nothing more than an awareness of the punishments the universe devises for its inhabitants." His outpouring "was a silent shriek of cosmic anger." When Muller speaks for himself, he declares, " . . . I'm the most human being there is, because I'm the only one who can't hid his humanity . . . . I speak for man. I tell the truth. I'm the skull beneath the face . . . . I'm all the garbage we pretend isn't there, all the filthy animal stuff, the lusts, the little hates, the sicknesses, the envies . . . ." [31]

Although Silverberg may well have wanted the protagonist of *The Man in the Maze* to serve as Everyman, that potential image is dulled by an ending that seems contrived, though to some degree it anticipates later novels. After a sequence of melodramatic action brings Muller out of the maze voluntarily, he goes to the aliens and realizes that they are probing his mind. Gladly he surrenders to them and knows that they are changing him. Although the significance of this for the future of mankind is not mentioned, Muller learns that he no longer exudes the aura that isolated him. Told that he can now return to Earth, he wonders whether or not "humanity [is] fit to consort with me." [32] And returns to Lemnos. This willful isolation negates any redemptive quality of the final encounter with the aliens.

When one tries to summarize the cumulative impact of "Flies," *Thorns*, "Passengers," and *The Man in the Maze*, one discovers that, like many contemporary writers working in the modes of social and psychological realism, Silverberg found himself confronted with the dilemma of man's tortured consciousness trapped within itself in a world seemingly without meaning for the individual. Like them, too, he sought to resolve the problem, both aesthetically and thematically. Two transitional novels from the period deserve notice. Although Silverberg has dismissed *To Open the Sky* (1967) as a "pseudo-novel constructed from five novelettes" published in Frederik Pohl's *Galaxy* in 1965 and 1966, [33] Russell Letson has called it "the book that signals the full emergence of the 'new' Silverberg . . . not only because of its use of characteristic images and motifs and its literary control; it also announces the themes that will dominate his work hereafter." [34] Such a judgment divorces the loosely structured *To Open the Sky* from the aforementioned works, to all of which it is artistically inferior; yet in that it emphasizes immortality, religious awakening, apocalypse, and extrasensory powers, it does indicate something of the new perspective which Silverberg sought to escape the dark vision of the more demanding works of the period. Like *Thorns* and *The Man in the Maze*, it loses some of its potential because of the objectivity of its point of view as well as its episodic nature. Opening with the statement "There was chaos on the face of the earth," its storyline traces the growth of a new religion founded by Noel Vorst from its emergence during "an apocalyptic time" [35] to the achievement of its founders' initial aims after almost a century (2077-2164). Its essence lies in "its scientific program," for Vorst has deliberately set out "to transform the world" to attain his obsessive dream, to "see mankind go to the stars." [36] Because the traditional religions have lost much of their relevance in a decadent world, Vorst has formulated one which adores the atom as the unifying principle and has enunciated "The Electromagnetic Litany" to celebrate "the stations of the spectrum." [37] What results is the skeleton of a novel: five disconnected, though obviously related moments in a century-long time-span which conveniently permits the protagonist of each novelette to retain a place in the narrative because each man has gained longevity, if not immortality. One senses that Silverberg is toying with the ideas that fascinate him; the genetic engineering of human beings so that they may dwell upon Venus; immortality; the development of extrasensory powers so that mankind may transcend the limitations of the human condition; the alteration of the molecular structure of the human brain; and, of course, the attainment of interstellar travel. Instead of a sustained dramatic sequence of action or a probing study of character, however, the reader listens to expository dialogue, especially in the final episode in which Vorst reveals how thoroughly he has manipulated people and the world itself to achieve his goal.

In the early days of the movement (the 1980's), for example, David Lazarus opposed Vorst, believing that he had brought about "a bluntly materialistic creed whose chief come-on was the promise of long (or eternal) life." [38] When Vorst began to seize political and economic control of Earth, Lazarus headed a schism, the Harmonists, who thought Vorst's methods were wrong. Lazarus disappears, supposedly assassinated by Vorst or his followers; his apparent martyrdom strengthens the Harmonists at a crucial time so that they soon control Venus, where they are free to develop their experiments in telekinesis. Some sixty years later Lazarus is found in a glass vault on Mars; Vorst's scientists resuscitate him so that he may assume command of the Harmonist movement.   Significantly, the *Book of Lazarus* does not "discredit" Vorst; Reynolds Kirby, a convert in the early period who has become Vorst's "alter ego," although he makes only random appearance in the narrative, cannot remember Lazarus as an intimate of Vorst's; and Lazarus himself reflects that his reappearance can only embarrass the Harmonists, whose mythos insists that he was fed into an electronic converter. [39] The result of the schism has been the independent development of both groups; Vorst's followers "have Earth and immortality," while the Harmonists "have Venus and teleportation." [40]

Kirby and the reader learn that Vorst "encouraged the Harmonist heresy" [41] because he was uncertain that man could gain the stars without the help of those having telekinetic power. At the end of the narrative, he departs Earth on a ship guided by the sensitives who can move freely in time and space, (the "espers") developed on Earth and powered by those having the power of telekinesis (the "pushers") developed on Venus.   At best Vorst is a shadow of Simeon Krug, whose ambitions control the action of *Tower of Glass* (1970).   Silverberg's pessimism is absent from *To Open the Sky*, but the narrative lacks a tone of affirmation. None of the protagonists of the individual novelettes understands the role he plays in Vorst's grandiose scheme, while Vorst himself can only hope that he has made the correct moves in his lengthy chess game.   Although his departure is eulogized by Kirby, who emphasizes that "the way was open" and that Vorst's ascension has given "lesser men" their turn, he remains unsure that humanity will "spill out across the heavens" to inherit the stars. [42]

Far more effective is the second of the transitional novels, *The Masks of Time* (1968), published in Britain as *Vornan-19* (1970). Its success stems largely from the greater artistry with which Silverberg handles his theme.   Presented as the first-person memoir of Leo Garfield—a professor of physics at the University of California-Irvine, whose specialty "concerns the time-reversal of subatomic particles" [43]—he supplies a skeptical point of view from which to judge Vornan-19, who has supposedly traveled back in time from 2999 and has materialized nude in Rome on Christmas Day, 1998. A skillful touch occurs in that Garfield must learn of Vornan's arrival second hand. First, Vornan's appearance disconcerts the world-wide cult of the Apocalypse—their demonstrations remind the reader of the movements and the criticism of the U.S. in the 1960's—which preaches that the decadent world will end with the millenium. Second, the cult hates him because he represents the future; yet even its members are attracted to him because he promises survival through an "epoch racked by fears of imminent extinction." [44] A third thread of action stems from Garfield's graduate student who is studying the atomic binding forces. He ceases his research because he is afraid that his work will make possible the release and control of unlimited energy, thereby bringing about "the end of our whole economic structure"; he cannot "assume the responsibility for overturning the world." [45] Yet he is drawn to Vornan, whose remarks imply that in his time such energy is available. So distraught is Garfield's student that for a time at least he wishes the Apocalyptists were right. [46]

The government insists that Garfield become one of a team of scientists accompanying Vornan throughout the United States and the Americas. Supposedly their primary function will be to determine his authenticity, but it becomes obvious that they are expected to protect him and to keep him from causing public disturbances. At first Garfield considers him a fraud, but one watches his judgment vacillate in the face of both biological and linguistic evidence as well as his own evaluation of Vornan's manner.

Vornan himself remains one of Silverberg's memorable creations. Certainly he serves as a highly effective means of satire, but he grows much more complex than a mere mask intended to voice criticism. To begin with, in a most off-handed way, he provides no more than bits and pieces of information about his own period. Yes, his people have reached the stars, there is no population problem; technology is available but kept in the background: "no wars. No nations. A simple, pleasant, happy world." [47] He reveals that there are "servitors . . . who do not have full human status because they are genetically other than human"; at times, however, he cannot—or refuses—to explain some aspect of his world because he is not a "scientist." [48] He is, of course, sexually promiscuous and cannot understand the workings of an automatic brothel in Chicago, partly because he cannot comprehend anyone not gaining pleasure from the sexual act. Two of the most effective satirical scenes succeed because of their humor. As a guest of the wealthy, eccentric Wesley Bruton, he attends a party at a fully automated house designed by an avant-guard architect and "considered a landmark of artistic accomplishment." He first reacts by asking if the "therapy" works; then he asserts that the "house—is a comedy itself" and tells the owner that he admires "the taste of your architect, his restraint, his classicism." But when Bruton asserts that there will be "Nothing to equal [the house] in the next thousand years" and asks directly whether or not it exists in Vornan's time as a "monument of the past," the time-traveler replies, " . . . I believe the primitive barbarity of this structure might have been offensive to those who lived in the Time of the Sweeping, when many things changed. Much perished then through intolerance." [49] He ends the evening by twisting the dials of the computer set-up so that the house runs out of control. More devastating is his inability to understand the workings of the New York Stock Exchange as its president tries to explain it to him; he suggests that the intricacies of corporations, stocks, the market, and even capitalism remain beyond him, much to the consternation of his informant, who wonders whether or not the whole world has gone Communist by Vornan's time. [50] At times one cannot decide whether Vornan is deliberately naive or intentionally withholding information. At one crucial point, however, he tries to make Garfield understand that he came to 1998 as a tourist, not as a scholar, and that in his own time he had no profession; moreover, he is no pioneer, for there have been many time-travelers, some of whom have held public office. Garfield refuses to believe him, but their conversation is cut short as they encounter a mob. Garfield does not immediately know whether that mob is made up of Apocalyptists "or those who sought Vornan to worship him." [51]

By the time that Vornan confides to Garfield in this manner, his role in the apocalyptic world of the end of the twentieth century has radically changed. During a television show devoted to a discussion of religion, Vornan had asked whether or not the panelists would like to hear what the scientists of the next thousand years had learned regarding the origin of human life. " . . . our planet was visited by explorers from another star," he tells them. "They did not land [because Earth] was without life . . . . They paused only long enough to jettison certain garbage [which] found its way into the sea, introducing certain factors that created a chemical disturbance and set in motion the beginning of the process . . . ." [52]

The "garbage" theory starts a controversy. For some it is blasphemy; for others, "The Word." Soon transcripts of all his "press conferences and media appearances" are released in "a quick flimsy book" entitled *The New Revelation*. Morton Fields, a scientist who has quit the committee, adds fuel with *The Newest*

Revelation, whose author neither claims Vornan is "literally divine" nor offers "a final opinion on the genuineness of his claim to have come from the future." Garfield asserts that he believes that Fields was suggesting that "we ourselves had made Vornan into a god. We had needed a deity to preside over us as we entered our new millenium, for the old gods had abdicated; and Vornan had come along to fill our void." [53]

One of Silverberg's accomplishments in the novel is that he permits Vornan to change, although the result is at best ambiguous. On the one hand, Vornan seems to sense something of this response and wishes to mingle with those who listen to him. On the other, he angers—perhaps dismays is a better word—Garfield by having a homosexual liaison with Garfield's graduate student. Thus in South America when Vornan begins to preach that his audience can "shape a paradise while you yet live," Garfield responds by calling him "mischievous" and wondering if such talk is "the sign of new malice in the making." [54] When Kralick, the government man who persuaded Garfield to join the committee and who supervises the tour, suggests that Vornan is a risk, Garfield suggests that he have the time traveler killed. Kralick protests, but he provides Vornan with a "crowd shield . . . an electronic sphere of force that surrounds the wearer" protecting him against mobs. [55] Vornan wears it in Rio, and Garfield accompanies him as they mingle with the crowd. The shield does not work; Vornan is torn to pieces by his adorers. Afterward, Garfield writes, "We have written the proper climax for the myth. When a young god comes among us, we slay him." [56] The ambiguity seems obvious. It is heightened by Garfield's asking Kralick why he permitted Vornan to have the shield and by his asserting, as he and Vornan move toward that final crowd, "It is given to few men to become gods in their own lifetimes." He concludes by speculating that humanity is "coming into a century of flame. I fear that I may live to see the Time of the Sweeping of which Vornan spoke." [57] Garfield himself speaks of ambiguities.

The Masks of Time must be regarded as an artistic success, although certainly not one of Silverberg's finest. By and large, he managed to contain his criticism and pessimism within Leo Garfield's narrative; in doing this, he showed that he could dramatize his anxieties, as he had in "Flies," *Thorns*, "Passengers," and *The Man in the Maze*, for example, instead of treating them as abstract ideas—grandiose plans—as he did in *To Open the Sky*. The flaw of the novel also lies with Garfield, for until the last possible moment he remains essentially the neutral—or judicious—observer. (At best his attitude vacillates until after the liaison between Vornan and the graduate student disgusts him; he does not come to a firm concept of Vornan in his own time or in relationship to the twentieth century, as witnessed by his refusal to believe that time travelers had intruded into history; and finally, he "comes to realize" too quickly. In short, the ambiguities overwhelm him.) While *The Masks of Time* does not share the dark vision of "Flies," *Thorns*, "Passengers," and *The Man in the Maze*, neither does it offer an acceptable resolution to the problems called up by Vornan's appearance and behavior. Like Garfield, he seemed unable to come up with a firm resolution. One cannot argue that the weaknesses of the two men strengthened the novel, for its ambiguities did not achieve the level of irony. Yet in its artistry, both in terms of technique and theme, *The Masks of Time* does point toward the major novels in which Silverberg found protagonists who could confront "the real anguish of life" and come away, however briefly, with an affirmative resolution.

NOTES

1. "MLA Forum: Science Fiction: The New Mythology," *Extrapolation*, 10 (May 1969), 102.
2. Ibid., p. 95.
3. Silverberg, "Sounding Brass, Tinkling Cymbal," pp. 28-29.
4. Thomas L. Wymer, "Perception and Value in Science Fiction," in *Many Futures, Many Worlds*, ed. Thomas D. Clareson (Kent, Ohio: Kent State University Press, 1977), pp. 1-13; Thomas D. Clareson, "Many Futures, Many Worlds," in *Many Futures, Many Worlds*, pp. 14-26.
5. Silverberg, "untitled headnote to 'Warm Man,'" *The Best of Robert Silverberg*, p. 32.
6. Silverberg, "Warm Man," pp. 41, 42.
7. Silverberg, "Warm Man," p. 44.
8. Silverberg, "Introduction," *The Seed of Earth*, pp. xi, xv.
9. Silverberg, *The Seed of Earth*, pp. 148, 157.
10. Silverberg, "Sounding Brass, Tinkling Cymbal," p. 28; "untitled headnote to 'To See the Invisible Man,'" *The Best of Robert Silverberg*, p. 48.
11. Silverberg, "untitled headnote to 'Flies,'" *The Best of Robert Silverberg*, p. 48.
12. Silverberg, "Flies," p. 83.
13. Silverberg, "Flies," p. 88.
14. Silverberg, "Flies," p. 91.
15. Silverberg, "Passengers," *The Best of Robert Silverberg*, p. 155.
16. Silverberg, "untitled headnote to 'Passengers,'" p. 150.
17. Silverberg, "Sounding Brass, Tinkling Cymbal," p. 32.
18. Ibid., p. 34.
19. Ibid., p. 33.
20. Ibid., p. 34.

21. Ibid., pp. 37, 38.
22. Silverberg, *Thorns* (New York: Ballantine Books, 1967), p. 12.
23. Ibid., p. 48.
24. Ibid., p. 17.
25. Clareson, ''The Fictions of Robert Silverberg,'' p. 9.
26. Silverberg, *Thorns*, p. 222, as cited by Clareson, p. 9.
27. Ibid., p. 169.
28. Clareson, ''The Fictions of Robert Silverberg,'' p. 8.
29. Silverberg, *The Man in the Maze* (New York: Avon Equinox Books, n.d.), p. 113, as cited by Clareson, p. 9.
30. Silverberg, *The Man in the Maze*, pp. 166, 167, as cited by Clareson, p. 9.
31. Silverberg, *The Man in the Maze*, pp. 114, 124, as cited by Clareson, p. 10.
32. Silverberg, *The Man in the Maze*, p. 187, as cited by Clareson, p. 12.
33. Silverberg, ''Sounding Brass, Tinkling Cymbal,'' p. 31.
34. Russell Letson, ''Introduction,'' *To Open the Sky* (Boston: Gregg Press, 1977), pp. v, x.
35. Silverberg, *To Open the Sky*, p. 27.
36. Ibid., pp. 189, 195, 25.
37. Ibid., [p. 11].
38. Ibid., p. 174.
39. Ibid., pp. 137, 153, 167-168, 175, 179.
40. Ibid., p. 134.
41. Ibid., p. 208.
42. Ibid., p. 222
43. Silverberg, *The Masks of Time* (New York: Ballantine Books, 1968), p. 9.
44. Ibid., p. 44.
45. Ibid., pp. 52-53.
46. Ibid., p. 170.
47. Ibid., p. 185.
48. Ibid., pp. 105, 160.
49. Ibid., pp. 107, 110, 111, 114.
50. Ibid., pp. 120-133.
51. Ibid., pp. 186-188.
52. Ibid., p. 174.
53. Ibid., pp. 199, 218.
54. Ibid., p. 241.
55. Ibid., p. 240.
56. Ibid., p. 251.
57. Ibid., pp. 243, 249, 252.

IV

THE MAJOR NOVELS: 1969 - 1976

Granted that some readers and critics prefer the fiction that Silverberg produced in the early days of his career. They make up a group which sees science fiction primarily as a form of adventure fiction in which mankind acts heroically—and successfully—on a cosmic stage. Essentially they have not liked much of the fiction resulting from such innovations as the new wave; increasingly, too, they have been a minority voice. Yet even those individuals who do not gain a personal satisfaction from Silverberg's later work will agree that his most provocative fiction comes from the 1960's and 1970's. (One recalls his succinct remark that *"Thorns* did not universally delight." [1]) His career can now be divided into four overlapping periods, for, as noted, his work has not exhibited any simplistic, linear development. The earliest period covered 1955-1959, an apprenticeship when he turned out fiction that by and large remained within the parameters of established magazine science fiction; 1960-1968, a time of transition when he reworked some of the earlier stories, but more importantly a time when his dissatisfaction and pessimism allowed a dark vision to dominate the best of his newest fiction; 1969-1976, almost a full decade when he deliberately experimented, both technically and thematically, in an attempt to discover how much science fiction could be expanded so that, like contemporary social and psychological realism, it could convey metaphorically statements about the condition of man and his society; and finally, beginning in 1979/1980, the discovery of Majipoor.

While no one would be so foolish as to call *Lord Valentine's Castle* (1980) a minor novel, and while some will argue that earlier works, like *Thorns* and *The Man in the Maze*, for example, deserve a place among his major novels, one can argue that the novels (and some of the shorter fiction) published between 1969 and 1976 delimit his major period because during those years he conducted his most deliberate experiments and attained the most consistent command of his material. On the other hand, there will be those who want to include such works as *The Masks of Time*, which failed to gain the Nebula award by only a few votes, [2] among the major novels. Let them make that judgment, but as suggested, for various reasons having to do with its artistry, it seems more a transitional work which helped to lay the foundation from which the major novels rose.

1. *Nightwings* (1969)

Nightwings (1969) is made up of three novellas originally published in *Galaxy* (little changed when combined into the novel): "Nightwings" (September 1968), which won a Hugo award as well as a Nebula nomination; "Perris Way" (November 1968); and "To Jorslem" (February 1969), which gained both Hugo and Nebula nominations. Perhaps not surprisingly, Silverberg has said little about this novel, perhaps because, as Brian W. Stableford, the ablest British critic of his fiction, has pointed out, Silverberg wrote the novel during the months immediately following the 1968 fire. Although Stableford has pointed out the "depth of personal feeling and an entirely private significance" apparent to him in the narrative, he has not elaborated on the "authenticity of the emotion" which he perceives in it; in his final judgment, however, "everything that Silverberg does in *Nightwings* he went on to do much better in other novels" of the 1970's. [3] From an acquaintance with Stableford, one infers that this verdict may well be rooted in personal preference, rising, in part, from Stableford's training and interests. He is presently a lecturer in sociology at Reading University.

In *Nightwings* Silverberg returned to the timeworn storyline of an Earth threatened by alien invaders. Stableford agrees that Silverberg achieved something very different from his earlier works dealing with the theme. [4] The impact of *Nightwings*, especially the lead novella, results from Silverberg's control of all elements of the story so that he produces a narrative that has a tone and an aesthetic distancing seemingly unique in his fiction. Countless individuals have judged it the most lyrical of his novels. It is also his first successful dramatization of a quest for redemption and transcendence, the theme that grows out of the first part of the narrative.

Silverberg excapes the travail of the late-twentieth century by casting the reader into an indefinite period of time, the Third Cycle of civilization, after Earth has fallen from the greatness of the Second Cycle, during which "epoch mankind spread out to the stars, and the stars came to mankind," while through such wonders as genetic engineering—applied both to humans and to animals—man exploited "the environment to the fullest [and] created a paradise on Earth." [5] Yet after "some thousands of years of glories beyond my capacity to comprehend," the powers of the Second Cycle "overreached themselves" as a result of "foolish arrogance" and "excessive confidence." [6] The catastrophic fall changed the very contours of the Earth. A Land Bridge joins the continent of Afreek to Talya, while only "scattered islands rising in two long strips from Earth Ocean—the remnants of the Lost Continents" [7] remind the narrator that the Americas have vanished beneath the sea.

Perhaps because the "Earth is a neglected world in a backwater of the universe," where "visitors from the stars" haggle with merchants in the markets of ancient Roum, [8] it has a medieval flavor to it both in the terms of cities instead of nations being the chief principalities and in that society as a whole is organized into guilds. The reader views everything through the eyes of the aged, first-person narrator, known initially simply as the Watcher. He takes his name from his guild, but he is much more than a passive observer; ritualistically, four times a day, he must project his consciousness far out into space to ascertain if enemy ships approach. Such a threat is part of the legacy of the Second Cycle; for more than a thousand years another race has coveted Earth "and owns it by treaty, and will some day come and collect." [9]

The Watcher comes to Roum with two companions: Avluela, one of those who has been given wings through genetic engineering so that she may be a Flier; and Gorman, the Changeling, a mutated monster who is guildless and therefore an outcast from society. Refused shelter in the hostelry of the Watchers, the three are taken under the protection of the Prince of Roum after he uses Avluela sexually. At last Gorman reveals that he has been sent to Earth as a military observer to help prepare for the invasion, which comes suddenly in the night after the Watcher declares that such a threat is "imaginary" and that his life has been wasted. The reader cannot yet appreciate the irony of the remark that the invaders "are most gentle. They have *collected* us." [10] The Watcher finds the Prince of Roum, blinded by Gorman supposedly in retaliation for his treatment of Avluela, and sets out with him for Perris. Now that his task as a Watcher is finished, the narrator wishes to join the guild of Rememberers, for he wants to learn of Earth's past. One incidental reference could easily be missed; yet it illustrates something of the way in which Silverberg's imagination works, as well as showing the manner in which his works are inter-related. At one point, almost in passing, Basil the Rememberer informs the others that his guild has found "the catacombs of Imperial Roum, and the rubble of the Time of Sweeping"; it is no accident, for later the narrator refers to the end of the Second Cycle as "a Time of Sweeping." [11] Not otherwise explained, the phrase nevertheless calls up *The Masks of Time* with its implications of drastic change. All in all, the opening sequence of *Nightwings* presents a world more richly textured than any Silverberg had yet created. One cannot help comparing it to the Urth of Gene Wolfe's *The Shadow of the Torturer* (1980).

The second part of the narrative, called "Among the Rememberers" in the novel, affords the Watcher—now called Tomis the Rememberer because he is an apprentice of the guild—an opportunity to search the data banks and discover what caused the downfall of the Second Cycle of civilization. When Earthmen reached the stars, the trauma of encountering ancient races "generated an aggressive urge to excel and surpass"; as material progress on Earth continued, there eventually developed the feeling that many aliens were inferior, worthy only of contempt. "Thus it was proposed to establish 'study compounds' on Earth for specimens of inferior races," but because of the "expense of collecting and maintaining the specimens," the compounds were soon opened as public "zoos for other intelligent species." They became "a major attraction, one of the wonders of the cosmos" so that other races overlooked "the amorality of the basic concept" to "share the pleasure of inspecting the prisoners." When a "roughly humanoid" race was discovered, a "collecting team acquired a breeding colony of these people." The humanoids protested, but lengthy diplomatic proceedings accomplished nothing. Angrily, the inhabitants of H362 threatened that one day they would conquer Earth and turn it "into a gigantic compound for its own people." [12] In short, they would collect humanity.

Their opportunity came after mankind attempted to gain "full control of the planetary climate." After centuries of preparation, involving greater expense than any other project in history, the weather machines began operation. "The result was devastation," including a shifting of the geographical poles, a lengthy glaciation of the northern hemisphere, and the sinking of the western continents. Some of the more powerful galactic races "took command" of Earth; in turn, the inhabitants of H362 reimbursed "Earth's receivers"—asking only, in return, "an assignment of all rights and claims to Earth." [13] Thus did they gain their revenge when they finally invaded Earth.

While Tomis has gained this knowledge, the blind Prince of Roum—wanted by the aliens because he was ruler, "a proscribed Dominator"—has had an affair with Olmayne, herself a Rememberer and the sponsor of Tomis. Her husband, Elegro, and the Prince quarrel. In an attempt to gain amnesty for the Prince, Tomis reveals to the aliens the existence of "an image recording of the compound in which your kidnapped ancestors lived while they were prisoners on Earth. It shows their sufferings in poignant detail. It is a superb justification for the conquest of Earth by H362." [14] The aliens agree. Not only does Tomis feel guilt at betraying his "Earthborn heritage" by thus serving the conquerors, but he is expelled from the guild of Rememberers. Moreover, his action has been in vain, for Elegro has slain the Prince, after which Olmayne killed her husband. She makes arrangements with the guild of Pilgrims so that she and Tomis can journey to Jorslem.

He reflects that the process of Watching "was a transcending of self"; on his way to Jorslem, with the aid of a starstone—a gem from one of the outer worlds which one must possess to qualify as a pilgrim—he again experiences a transcendence, becoming one with all of those pilgrims moving toward Jorslem; he feels purified as a result of the experience. [15] Once in Jorslem, acknowledging that he seeks "Renewal. Redemption," he senses that he has somehow linked with the mind of the person examining him to decide whether or not he is worthy of renewal. Having been made young again—Olmayne does not survive the process—Tomis first is reunited with Avluela, who tells him that she has always loved him and joins the new guild of Redeemers. As all of his companions urge him telepathically to join together with them—to enter them—transcendence again takes place: " . . . I knew this was something wholly new on Earth, not merely the founding of a new guild but the initiation of a new cycle of human experience, the birth of the Fourth Cycle upon this defeated planet . . . . They put a vision before me of a transformed planet . . . . They showed me an Earth that had been purged of its ancient sins." [16] Once individual isolation is ended—so that "each of us is part of every other one of us"—there will be no further suffering; even the vengeful alien conquerors will be absorbed into the new spiritual unity.

Not even *Across a Billion Years* had risen to such a view of mankind's future. *Downward to the Earth*, being serialized when *Nightwings* saw book publication, did not attain the same certainty that the guild of the Redeemers achieved. The apocalyptic vision of Tomis the Rememberer, who had been Watcher and Pilgrim, remains the simplest, yet most complete statement of affirmation in Silverberg's fiction.

2. *Downward to the Earth* (1970)

Nightwings and *Downward to the Earth* (1970) must be considered companion volumes, for incidents, characters, and themes echo from one novel to the other. Although both novels employ the motif of contact between human and alien to explore the themes of redemption and transcendence, significant differences result from several factors. In *Nightwings* humanoid aliens who seek revenge for being humiliated by mankind take possession of a decadent Earth; in *Downward to the Earth*, a remorseful Edmund Gundersen journeys to Belzagor, known to Earthmen as

Holman's World, where for at least a decade he served as a colonial administrator. Whereas Tomis, as first-person narrator, reveals and participates in what will undoubtedly become a spiritually renewed world, Gundersen indulges in a private quest which will, hopefully, somehow cleanse him of the deep sense of guilt haunting him since he left Belzagor eight years earlier. Thus, Silverberg uses Tomis as a means of opening up a panorama, while through the use of the third-person point of view in *Downward to the Earth*, he dramatizes and focuses ever more closely on the consciousness and sensibility of his individual protagonist. In both novels physical action is conspicuously minimized. They are both quests, but the effect of each is different.

Silverberg has explained that in February, 1969, he had "visited the great game parks of East Africa" and had come away with the idea for a novel "set in a time of diminishing imperialist exploitation, in which the heroes were the elephants." He went on to say that "the transcendental element in my work," already visible in *The Man in the Maze* and "more conspicuous" in *Nightwings*, "now came to play a major role" in the new novel. [1] He has also acknowledged his indebtedness to both Kipling and Conrad, especially the latter's *Heart of Darkness*. A number of matters—most obviously the name Kurtz—tie *Heart of Darkness* and *Downward to the Earth* together. Gundersen's venture into the Mist Country parallels Marlow's journey into the interior. Also, "Silverberg explores man's encounter with alien intelligence much in the manner that Conrad explored the European encounter with the jungle (the primitive world)." [2] Yet one must hasten to emphasize that Silverberg remained his own man; he produced an adaptation (not a slavish imitation) of Conrad's narrative. Gundersen is not Kurtz; nor are the aliens the oppressed natives of Africa.

He had not left his post voluntarily; rather, he had been removed only after Earth deliberately terminated a lengthy period of imperialism by returning the colonized planets to their indigenous, intelligent species: in the case of Belzagor to the elephantine nildoror and the seemingly secondary sulidoror, baboon-like creatures whose relationship to the nildoror men have never been able to comprehend. Gundersen returns to this jungle world because he is haunted by a sense of sin, rising in part because men—he himself included—used these intelligent beings as servants and beasts of burden. Upon his arrival, while talking with one of the few humans who did not leave the planet (he now acts as guide for those human tourists who regard Belzagor as a giant zoo, if they think of it in terms other than lost profits), Gundersen blunders into the error common to many of Silverberg's characters. He complains that as an official it was his "duty" to guide them

. . . . Futile though it was to think that a bunch of animals who don't have a written language, who don't—" [3] He stops, "horrified" that he has called them "Animals."

The core of Gundersen's guilt stems from a single incident. Suddenly confronted by a crisis when a dam broke, he pressed seven nildoror into a work detail; by doing so, he prevented them from going into the Mist Country to participate in the religious ceremony of rebirth. That ceremony involves a mystic compulsion on the part of the nildoror, for they have no control over its timing. The need comes upon them. If they do not answer the "summons" when it occurs, they cannot be sure that they will ever again be called to rebirth. Its importance to them may be seen in that they refer to their most respected elders as "the many-born." At the time of the incident, one cannot be certain how much Gundersen understands of its significance. Threatening to kill the group if they do not join those working on the dam, he actually did burn one of them with a fusion torch to save face when his victim says that he pities Gundersen. Since then, he has brooded over the concept of "rebirth"; for him, it has become synonymous with redemption. Thus he seeks permission to join a party of nildoror now undertaking the trek to the Mist Country. After he has eaten and danced with them, he is allowed to join the pilgrimage.

As he goes northward toward the Mist Country, he meets various humans who have been captured by Belzagor. He finds one couple, hardly alive, who have become hosts for a parasitic fungus and orders them killed. He meets his former lover, Seena, at Shangri-La Falls. She has surrendered to a gelatinous amoeba which embraces her belly and loins, though it releases her upon command. Her husband conjures up memories of *Heart of Darkness*, for he is Kurtz, lying ill and deformed and recalling the "horror" of his experience. [4] Long ago he milked serpents of their venom and fed that venom to the nildoror, himself, his companions at his outpost, and even Gundersen. They danced crazily, hallucinating. The venom is an essential drug. In a diluted form, it is used on Earth to regenerate organs; at full strength on Belzagor, it is an essential part of the process of rebirth. "Thus Kurtz profaned the most important rite of the nildoror religion, treating it as sport and entertainment" [5]: a travesty. When Kurtz sought to undergo rebirth, he emerged in the monstrous form which Gundersen finds Seena caring for. Warned by her that he will "cease to be human" if he participates in the ceremony, Gundersen replies, "I've tried being human for quite a while. Maybe it's time to try something else." [6] His response constitutes "the most explicit condemnation of man made by any of Silverberg's protagonists" to that date. [7]

Not only does Kurtz remind one of Conrad, but he also evokes Olmayne of *Nightwings*, who was so corrupt that she could not survive "renewal." Yet Gundersen will not be deterred, especially after he learns that the nildoror and the sulidoror—complementary species both physically and spiritually—are transformed from one to the other periodically so that "for those who merit it, life will have no end." [8] Moreover, each individual retains all knowledge from previous cycles. Uncertain what will happen to him, particularly since mankind has no complementary species like the sulidoror, Gundersen asks for transformation. (Although he is not made young again, the process itself reminds one somewhat of Tomis's renewal). Alone during rebirth, Gundersen experiences a spiritual oneness not only with the nildoror and sulidoror but also with "other Earthborn souls, as free as his . . . ." [9]

Although *Nightwings* remains the simplest, yet most complete affirmation regarding the future of mankind, *Downward to the Earth* achieves something more. In it Silverberg suggests the telepathic and spiritual unity of all intelligent life-forms, whatever their outward appearances. In this he reminds one of the work of Clifford D. Simak. Furthermore, by focusing the narrative upon the consciousness and spiritual growth of Gundersen, Silverberg has drawn one of his most memorable characters. Yet the final effect of the novel is one of promise more than of fulfillment, for Gundersen assumes a messianic role, telling his companions that he must go south to help Kurtz and then "the others," who remain deformed, imprisoned in their humanity.

Surprisingly, neither novel was reviewed widely when first published [10]; indeed, critical study of Silverberg did not become popular until after he announced his retirement from the field in 1975. As will be shown, there emerges a second element of irony —which in itself indicates the complexity of Silverberg's thought and, perhaps, his inability to arrive at a simple answer to the concerns which plagued him. As he worked on these two novels in which transcendence triumphs, he also wrote what may well be his single finest piece of fiction, the short story, "Sundance" (*F&SF*, June 1969), in which the world of his protagonist, Tom Two Ribbons, is reduced to chaos.

3. *Tower of Glass* (1970)

Two problems to which Silverberg addressed himself again and again are the nature of the universe itself—that is the nature and effect of determinism, which he was to treat most fully in *The Stochastic Man* (1975)—and the inability of individuals to communicate. In a sense each of his major narratives exemplifies a variation of his treatment of these central themes. When his emphasis lies with the incomprehensible, brutal nature of the universe, his dark vision prevails. More frequently, however, he has dealt with individual isolation resulting from the inability to communicate. The dramatization of either or both of these themes has produced that sense of alienation that so many critics have emphasized as an element of contemporary science fiction.

Both *Nightwings* and *Downward to the Earth* overcame that sense of estrangement—the desire both for release from the poverty of the human condition and thus for redemption—through the triumph of a transcendental experience bringing with it a feeling of unity. Such an answer collapsed in *Tower of Glass* (1970), which Silverberg has called one of his two novels "closer to pure science fiction, the exhaustive investigation of an extrapolative idea, than anything else I have written." [1] Although praising many aspects of the work, in speaking of the "ultimate science fiction novel" as "the satisfying link of character and idea," James Gunn regards the novel as "an interesting failure, though in its own right it is a rich, exciting, and rewarding novel that belongs with the best the genre has produced." [2] When Gunn was asked during the summer of 1982 what he considered to be the flaws of the novel, he replied that he did not think that Silverberg had completely fulfilled what he set out to do; as he wrote in his analysis of the novel, "the reader is left with a handful of unanswered questions." Such a response may exemplify the intentional fallacy, or, at least by implication, may indicate that Gunn would have handled the material in a different manner had he written the novel. [3]

Tower of Glass portrays a twenty-third century world dominated by the figure of Simeon Krug, whose accomplishments and desires shape its action. More than any other protagonist, he is Silverberg's Frankenstein, for essentially the narrative becomes a study of the creator and his creatures and the consequences of their relationship. His world is structured around "a small, culturally homogeneous human elite" living in affluence and capable of instantaneous travel anywhere in the world as a result of the system of "transmats"; the humans are "served by computers, mechanical robots, and hordes of obliging androids." [4] It came into being because as a youth Krug had begun to create androids from vats. " . . . growing up miserable in a town in Illinois with grass in the middle of its streets," fatherless, his mother hooked on "dream drugs," the embittered, lonely teenager had turned his "rage" outward. Because he showed a "remarkable intuitive grasp of the structure of things," he found financial backers, becoming a "new Thomas Edison," thinking, *I show you what I can do, I get even with you all!* " [5]

Even as he is "diddling with the nucleic acid . . . dipping his hands deep into tubs of slime, hooking together the protein chains," he grows obsessed with the findings of space-probes sent to the nearest stars, for they return without evidence of "advanced life-forms out there." Yet he wonders "how man can be alone in the universe if one man himself can make life?" Having shown mankind what he can do, he dreams of reaching "the people in the stars," of announcing his name to them. Thus he views his "whole life as a single process, tending without detour or interruption toward this one goal." [6]

Were this megalomania not enough, the reader recognizes the inevitability of a tragic confrontation when Krug says of the androids: " . . . *Things*. Factory-made things. I was building a better kind of robot. I wasn't building men." [7] On this opinion rests the first major irony of *Tower of Glass*. Dismissing his creatures as mere artifacts, Krug allows his loneliness to feed upon the reception of signals—numerical patterns; 2-4-1, 2-5-1, 3-1—apparently coming from the planetary nebula NGC 7923, a system in Aquarius which has undergone something like a nova. If intelligent beings exist there, they must take some unimaginable form because of the "fantastically strong radiation." Yet Krug's imagination has conjured up a pastoral, idyllic world whose people "moved through the groves and vales of their paradise, probing the mysteries of the cosmos, speculating on the existence of other civilizations, at last sending their message to the universe. He had seen them opening their arms to the first visitors from Earth, saying, 'Welcome, brothers, welcome.'" [8] Although his body "rotted . . . the mind within soared to the farthest galaxies . . . . His universe now revolved about the quest to make reply." The idea of the aliens as monstrosities may have lessened his hope of finding a father-figure, but Krug insists that *"I plan to say, Hello, hello . . . . we wish no longer to be alone in the cosmos."* [9] To accomplish his end, he has employed innumerable androids, supervised by Alpha Thor Watchman, to erect a giant tower west of Hudson Bay, from which he may send forth his message.

In an obvious parallel to the civil rights movement in the United States at that time, Silverberg has had a minority of the androids form the Android Equality Party (AEP) in an effort to change the law's concept of them as property instead of persons and to gain representation in Congress. Although Krug "had chosen to create synthetic human beings, not mere machines," he himself calls this group, "malcontents," declaring that they "think it's black slavery all over again. But it isn't. It isn't. The others know that. They're content. Thor Watchman is content." [10] Here lies the second major point of irony, for Krug does not realize that the majority of androids worship him. One of Silverberg's major artistic achivements—in any of his fiction—is the creation of the androids' bible, which opens: "In the beginning there was Krug, and He said, Let there be Vats, and there were Vats. And Krug looked upon the Vats and found them good." [11]

Through the android, Thor Watchman, the reader learns that those who believe expect Krug to deliver them from servitude. Watchman knows "that a time of redemption is to come." [12] When a representative of the AEP is accidentally killed, Watchman despairs, wondering about "the hope of redemption . . . the mercy of the Maker" [13]; he enlists the aid of the lovely Alpha Lilith Meson, the lover of Krug's son, Manuel. (One could dwell upon the complexity of this symbolism, beginning with the idea of God the Father as creator and God the Son as redeemer. In addition, although Krug has made the androids with genitalia, he has rendered them sterile so that the development of a full-fledged sexuality permitting reproduction has become a dream of the androids. For a human to have sexual intercourse with an android is judged a perversion, especially by Krug.)

Manuel allows Lilith to lead him to "Gamma City," a refuge beneath Copenhagen, where the androids huddle together secretly, taking care of their "brothers" who have been ostracized because they have emerged malformed from the vats. In this underworld Manuel first learns that the androids worship his father. When told, Krug first dismisses it as of no concern to him and then admits that it "sickens" him, but he turns the incident around so that he can disparage Manuel for "laying with something out of a vat." [14] After Manuel has given him the android bible to read, Krug commands Thor Watchman to join him in the so-called shunt room to undergo a process whereby individuals may briefly touch the consciousness of one another. To gain emotional intensity, as he has throughout the novel, Silverberg shifts the point of view so that the reader sees the ensuing episode from the view of Watchman. The refusal of Krug "to accept godhead" as well as his "total dismissal of android aspirations" overwhelms Watchman [15]; he initiates a revolt by allowing the tower to crumple as a result of thawing the tundra. Krug kills him. He flees to his starship and "begins his journey at last" [16] as the cities of Earth burn, with Manuel standing helpless by the fallen tower. One need not belabor the symbolism. Surely the final image evokes the concept "of an indifferent god abandoning his creation to seek other worlds to toy with." [17] Whatever else one says of *Tower of Glass*, one must acknowledge that in it Silverberg more nearly achieves a metaphorical level than he does in most of his other works. Moreover, the novel becomes one of the most effective expressions of his dark vision.

4. *A Time of Changes* (1971)

In retrospect, one does not understand why *A Time of Changes* (1971) should be, thus far at least, the *only* novel by Silverberg to win a Nebula Award. Brian Stableford has quite properly pronounced it "inferior . . . to most of the other novels which he produced in that period" and suggests that the award was given "partly in recognition that *Downward to the Earth* and *Tower of Glass* had failed to win in the previous year." [1] Comparing it to Ayn Rand's *Anthem* (1946), Silverberg has said that he found himself "embarked on a novel in which it was forbidden for any character to refer to himself in the first person," adding that he wanted to portray a society dominated by a "dour, ritualized, formalized pseudo-modesty that conceals furious *macho* self-assertiveness." He went on to say that the novel was his "response to all that had happened in the last years of the 1960's" as well as a "record of that inner upheaval" that he himself experienced as the new decade began and he tried to decide whether or not he should leave New York for California. [2] Significantly, perhaps, this is as personal as Silverberg was to get in any of the introductions he wrote for the new paperback reprints of his novels in the late 1970's; in "Sounding Brass, Tinkling Cymbal," for example, he had simply mentioned that the novel had won a Nebula.

In a sense his statement regarding his technical task is misleading, for *A Time of Changes* is told in the first-person as the "autobiography" of its protagonist, Kinnall Darivall, the younger son of the hereditary septarch of the province of Sella on the northern continent, Valada Borthan. As he begins to write, he refers to his use of the pronoun "I" as "Obscene! Obscene!" Yet he has deliberately chosen this manner of narration as a final gesture in his conscious rebellion against the society in which he was raised, married, had a family, and knew power as an official of the Port Justiciary in the province of Manneran.

Centuries earlier colonists from Earth had settled the planet Borthan as a refuge where they could preserve their strong religious beliefs. They signed a Covenant that has rigidly governed the lives and manners of their descendants in an essentially feudal society. (Those who did not sign went to the southern continent, Sumara Borthan; since then, there has been little or no commerce between the continents.) Darivall reveals that "we are forbidden by custom to make our souls known to others." Thus the most grievous sin is that of "*selfbaring*," for the people have been taught that speaking "excessively of oneself . . . leads inevitably to self-indulgence, self-pity, and self-corruption; . . . we are prohibited even from using words like 'I' or 'me' in polite discourse." The only relief that an individual has from such "constricting solitude" is the act of confession to priests—the so-called "drainers"—or at a more superficial level governed by "etiquette" the exchange of confidences with one's bondbrother or bondsister, relationships often arranged by one's parents, as in Darivall's case, before a child is born. [3] In such a society, of course, the word "love" is unspoken, if indeed it is understood.

Against this background, after his father is killed in a hunting accident, Darivall flees Sella when his brother becomes Septarch to avoid a power struggle, if not assassination. The father of his bondsister, Halum, gives him a position in the Justiciary in Manneran, and although he has harbored a secret longing for Halum (a physical relationship with one's bond-kin is the second deadliest sin), he marries her sister Loimel as a kind of surrogate, and, of course, he has an unhappy life with her.

Particularly because the retrospective narration both concentrates upon Darivall's state of mind and removes the action from the dramatic here-and-now, the storyline is thin. After telling the reader that his "authority and responsibility" have increased "year by year," he introduces Schweig, "a commercial man," one of the few Earthmen to visit Borthan, and then admits that in his youth he dreamed of Earth. This allows Schweig to criticize the earlier civilization of Earth—" . . . their selfishness . . . . Their lack of concern for the generations to come. They filled the world with themselves and used everything up."—adding, "Ancient Earth made mistake after mistake, and choked itself in error, so that you would be spared from having to pass through the same fires and torments . . . . Earth died to redeem you starfolk from sin. How's that for a religious notion?" [4] More importantly, since he is an atheist, he is both envious and critical of the religious fervor of Borthan society, suggesting that its citizens glorify the self through "living apart from one another, each in the castle of his skull"; yet what eats at him is "the impact of knowing one is entirely alone in the universe." [5] He proposes that Darivall share with him a Sumaran drug which permits one to link himself to the mind of another. They take the drug, and Darivall is converted to its use, especially after Schweig says that he loves the Borthan prince. His declaration has no sexual connotation; it is a love based upon compassion, empathy. Together they travel to Sumara, Borthan to obtain a larger supply. While there, they participate in a ceremony with some of the primitive natives: "We were dissolved into one another. We were dissolved in love . . . . If you would know more than that you would have to glimpse what it is to be released from the prison of your skull." Darivall immediately envisions himself as "the evangelist. I was the new prophet. I was the messiah of openness." [6]

Schweig and he go their separate ways, but Darivall does try to convert various citizens—most of them strangers—to his new belief by sharing the drug with them. He shares it with Noim Condorit, his bondbrother, and with Halum. By then, he is already sought by the authorities, and her suicide seals his fate. He flees to the desert where he writes his autobiography. Noim comes to try to help him escape, but Darivall will not resist arrest; instead, he gives Noim the manuscript, hoping that he will read it and continue the work of conversion which he attempted to begin. Hallucinating as a result of using the drug alone, Darivall envisions Noim's success and instructs the reader, "Go and seek. Go and touch. Go and love. Go and be open. Go and be healed." [7] Silverberg has declared that some of his "straight friends misunderstood the book, thinking it was merely a tract urging wider and wilder use of psychedelic drugs. That wasn't my intention at all . . . ." [8] That he felt he had to make such an explanation is in itself a comment upon the work. Certainly he was dealing with familiar materials, but unlike the successful *Nightwings* and *Downward to the Earth*, for example, he took too close a perspective of the theme, among other things choosing the wrong narrative point of view. Despite the intensity of Darivall's emotions and despite the skill in creating so repressive a society, Silverberg did not make the act of transcendence convincing. One might say instead, perhaps, that the final vision of Darivall's is not an effective affirmation. There is neither the simplicity of *Nightwings* nor the hope of *Downward to the Earth*. In that fact lies the irony of the Nebula Award.

5. *Son of Man* (1971)

Silverberg has called *Son of Man* (1971) "my strangest, most individual book . . . a dream-fantasy of the far future, with overtones of Stapledon and Lindsay's *Voyage to Arcturus* and a dollop of psychedelia that was altogether my own contribution." [1] Stableford has defined it as "a surreal allegory" that "remains science fiction because the order of things reflected in its symbology is an evolutionary scheme rather than a theological one"; at least until 1980 it had remained his "personal favourite." [2] Although critics and reviewers gave it little notice when it first appeared, subsequently it has been generally regarded as his most lyrical and formless novel. There is no storyline as such. Silverberg projects his protagonist—Clay—far ahead in the "time-flux," where he awakens alone, lost, and hungry. Almost immediately he meets Hanmer—"not human" though "the kinship is apparent"—who will be his most frequent companion. By touching Clay, Hanmer relieves his hunger and announces, "We love you. We bid you welcome." [3] When Clay asks him how he speaks "my language" and insists that there are many languages, Hanmer replies, "When mind touches mind . . . communication is immediate and absolute. Why did you need so many ways of speaking to one another?" [4] This is merely the first encounter between Clay and innumerable descendants of man who have taken various shapes; some, like the Eaters, terrible to behold; others, like Quoi—*"an enemy of Wrong"*—capable of change. It is also the initial statement of the pervasive theme: transcendental unity. For example, Clay "opens his soul to" the female, Ninameen, as he attempts to show her artifacts from his period of time. Again, during the rite of the Opening of the Earth—when Clay can literally "see" the creatures who have burrowed beneath the ground and the roots of plants, as well as "the subterranean rocks and levels of stratification"—he dances with Hanmer, Ninameen, and their companions as they chant, "I am love . . . . I am love . . . . Love . . . . I am love." At its conclusion, he realizes that "He has never known such joy before." [5] To make Clay's sensations and experiences more immediate, Silverberg emloys the present tense throughout the novel.

Repeatedly Clay acknowledges that he represents man at an early stage of evolution. When Quoi asks if he may "examine" Clay's way of life, the "demonstration" becomes an incident in which Clay picks up a girl along a thruway, takes her to a motel, and has sexual intercourse with her; during the episode, she identifies herself as "Quoi." [6] Many of the beings, including Clay, are able to assume either the male or female role in their sexual encounters. The novel becomes a pastiche of such sexual/transcendental encounters as the characters seek to merge, to gain unity. Yet Hanmer and Ninameen leave him. When he is told that they seek to escape him because he carries within himself "a great cold wad of cruelty and ugliness" that hurts his companions, he understands that he must "experience the whole history of his race. He will take all of the world's anguish into himself." He embraces those whom he meets, including Hanmer and Ninameen, saying, "Give me your fear. Give me your hate. Give me your doubt . . . . I am Clay. I am love." [7] Thus does Clay become the redeemer. Perhaps the merit of the novel can best be measured by the fact that it has not yet had a hard cover edition. More importantly, during the late 1970's when Silverberg arranged new editions of many of his novels, including with each a new introduction, he omitted *Son of Man*.

6. *The World Inside* (1971)

The World Inside (1971) again exemplifies the difficulty of dating Silverberg's work, for it grew from the short story, "A Happy Day in 2381," which he wrote in 1968, [1] although it was not published until 1970 in Harry Harrison's *Nova 1*. The other "loosely related short stories" [2] brought together in this novel were also published in 1970 and 1971, but one cannot be absolutely certain of their dates of composition and sequence except to infer that they built upon the premises originally advanced in "A Happy Day in 2381."

60

Silverberg regards the novel as one of the two works "closer to pure science fiction" than anything else he had written because of its "exhaustive examination" of the consequences of overpopulation. It is his most explicit dystopia. Instead of a close concentration upon the sensibility of a single protagonist, he moves among a number of related characters to explore most fully the practices of the "post privacy society" inhabiting Urbmon 116, a self-contained unit, a thousand stories tall, housing more than 800,000 individuals. It is made up of twenty-five city units ranging from Reykjavik on the bottom to Louisville on top; moreover, as implied by the city divisions, it is a stratified culture in which workers do not mix with the academic levels because it "would make everyone unhappy." [3] Its inhabitants marry early—the boys at twelve, the girls at thirteen, although the precocious, like Siegmund Kruven, begin their sexual activities at seven or eight.

Urbmon 116 is one of fifty-one urban monads comprising the Chipitts (Chicago-Pittsburgh) constellation, which houses some forty million of Earth's total population of seventy-five billion. Beginning in the twenty-second century, terrestrial society solved the problem of overpopulation by two methods. First, rather than continuing the wasteful horizontal expansion of the old urban centers, society began to build upward, appropriately enclosing its citizens in a three-kilometer-tall erection. Second, instead of trying in any way to limit population growth, it embraced the worship of fertility: "We hold life sacred. Making new life is blessed. One does one's duty to god by reproducing." [4] It is, of course, a sexually permissive society in which "night-walking"—preferably in one's own city unit—to find at random a sexual partner has become the most acceptable means of releasing minor tensions. It is also bisexual: "My wife is available to you, as am I. Within the Urbmon it is improper to refuse any reasonable request, so long as no injury is involved." [5]

Unlike Harry Harrison's *Make Room, Make Room* (1966), however, *The World Inside* is not a cautionary tale of gloom and doom. Silverberg gains his impact, at least in "A Happy Day in 2381," through a delightful irony. He achieves this through his choice of narrator, Charles Mattern, a "sociocomputator," a devoted advocate of the urban monad culture. On this particular day, he must explain the workings of Urbmon 116 to a visitor from Venus, Nicanor Gortman, as they tour this "Utopia." [6] Thus Silverberg's satire and irony are immediately strengthened because the reader recognizes that he has adapted the structure of the classic utopian tale to his own ends. Except for an occasional question or innocent "excruciatingly impolite statement," [7] Gortman remains passive. In response to Gortman's questions, not only does Mattern declare that "we cannot allow" wild animals to exist on Earth, but he also explains that "Life on Earth is quite bearable . . . . There is no need of escape literature." [8] After all, as a sociocomputator, he is one of the few allowed to go outside the urbmon unit; he is a sophisticate; he studies "offworld journals for *amusement*. And to obtain a necessary parallax, you know, for my work." [9]

Mattern is also a data bank, enthusiastically praising the city of Prague—perhaps the 117th floor—whose families average 9.9 children ("littles") crowded into a single room. And so the information pours out, creating a vivid detailed impression of the world Silverberg has created. The success of the portrait results from the self-assuredness Mattern initially exhibits. Yet he himself reveals the basic horror underlying his society's solution to its basic problem when he unwittingly mocks the rationality upon which classical utopias have based their societies: "To be human is to meet challenges through the exercise of intelligence, right? . . . We could limit births [in a world free of disease and war], but that would be sick, a cheap anti-human way out . . . . And so we go on and on, multiplying joyously." [10]

The only action comes when one of the citizens goes "flippo," accosting his pregnant wife with a fabricator torch. Mattern would ask the crazed man, "Why do you suddenly repudiate the principles on which—" [11] but the youth must be physically overcome by Mattern and a troop of school children chanting hymns. The police immediately condemn him to "erasure" and expel him through the "chute." Gortman looks stunned; Mattern reminds him that such things do happen. Although the incident reminds Mattern of his brother, "Jeffrey the unadaptable . . . who had to be given to the chute," he decides that it has been a happy day, as he goes nightwalking.

Thus, it is the character of Mattern that makes the story work. None of the others succeeds so well because Silverberg begins to investigate the malcontents. Auria Houston must go to the "moral engineers" when she cannot face the fact that she and her husband have been selected by lot to uproot themselves and move to the new Urbmon 158. Dillon Chrimes, a member of the cosmos musical group, gets high on multiplexers so that telepathically he encompasses everyone in the structure; despite his initial "ecstasy," however, when he comes down, he finds himself questioning the premises of the society. Jason Quevedo and his wife think of themselves as "throwbacks" because they feel jealous of one another's sexual escapades. His wife's brother is arrested and condemned to the chute because he leaves the urbmon. Silverberg gives most attention to Siegmund Kluver, an ambitious youth who rises to power in the Louisville Access Annex before he is twenty. Over-serious and sensitive, he is disillusioned when he sees those who rule the urbmon indulge themselves in an orgy on one of the holidays. Feeling isolated and alone, he commits suicide.

Although such characters tie *The World Inside* to his other works, it stands unique among the later novels because of its satire. "A Happy Day in 2381," particularly, comes as a welcome relief from his usual examination of the tortured protagonists of his fiction.

7. *The Second Trip* (1972)

Sometime early in the 1970's Silverberg has acknowledged that "it was becoming impossible for me to take the stuff of science fiction seriously any more—all those starships and androids and galactic empires"; he lost his belief in the "great themes" of the field, although they retained "powerful metaphorical value for me." [1] The resultant minimizing of science-fiction parapher-nalia is nowhere more evident than in *The Second Trip* (1972), serialized a year earlier in *Amazing Stories*; he has described it as "a rough and brutal novel of double identity." [2]

In *To Live Again* (1969) he had treated the theme of multiple consciousness in a very traditional science-fiction manner. The Scheffling Process allows one to fuse the mind of a dead person into one's own consciousness; the story turns on an involved struggle to obtain the mind of a financial genius. In *The Second Trip*, Silverberg dramatizes the Jekyll-and-Hyde confrontation, to which he alludes specifically. [3] After four years of treatment, Paul Macy emerges from the Rehab Center; his personality has been constructed to take the place of that of Nathaniel Hamlin, a psycho-sculptor who had been both a genius and a rapist. Con-demned by society, Hamlin's mind is supposedly erased and Macy's consciousness put in its place. But Macy's chance meeting with Lissa Moore, who had been Hamlin's mistress and the model for his *Antigone 21*, somehow triggers Hamlin into existence again because she is a telepath.

In sharp contrast to most of his other fiction, *The Second Trip* gives almost no attention to the external world—perhaps because it takes place in New York City early in the twenty-first century. A secondary element of the narrative is the running argument be-tween Macy and Dr. Gomez of the Rehab Center, who refuses to believe that Hamlin can still exist but does finally admit that "We all make mistakes." [4] The primary thrust centers upon the dialogues between Macy and Hamlin as they argue for possession of their shared body. Lissa—who can even hear the animals at the zoo—becomes the catalyst of the action. Driven almost mad by the ESP—"She picks up voices—half the time she doesn't know who she is—she has to hide from people, to shield herself" [5]—she several times saves Macy when Hamlin is about to take control. Although she hides from Macy, at the critical time she uses her power to destroy Hamlin, though that action costs her both the loss of her ESP and the collapse of her personality to an infantile state. The novel ends as Macy calls Dr. Gomez, hoping that Lissa may be restored so that they can take a "second trip. The good one, maybe." In that Silverberg strips the narrative to its barest essentials—the conflict between the men and the girl—it is simultaneously the slightest of his novels and, despite Macy's final hope, perhaps the one which leaves the reader with the greatest sense of despair, at least to that date. However that may be, *The Second Trip* was the portent of things to come.

8. *The Book of Skulls* (1972)

Just as one understands something of Silverberg's development through contrasting *To Live Again* and *The Second Trip*, so, too, does one see that same line emerge in the differences between *Recalled to Life* (1958, 1962, 1971) and *The Book of Skulls* (1972). Both deal with the theme of immortality. One is tempted to infer that the 1971 rewriting of the earlier novel may well represent Silverberg's last orthodox treatment of a major science-fiction theme. Like *To Live Again*, *The Book of Skulls* concentrates upon a process, this one developed by Beller Laboratories in 2033. If a body has sustained no brain damage, the laboratory can restore an individual's life within twenty-four hours of death. James Harker has been hired to sell the idea to the public, the church, and the government. He finally has no alternative but to undergo the process himself to prove its feasibility. A flutter of optimism makes itself heard when he speculates that "a new era" has begun in which death "has lost much of its finality" and man must write "a new code of laws . . . a new ethics." [1]

The Book of Skulls (1972) could not differ more radically from *Recalled to Life* than it does. In the library of a university, Eli, a Jewish intellectual, finds a manuscript supposedly written by members of a secret sect called the Keepers of the Skull. It promises immortality to its readers. The implications of a newspaper article send Eli and his three roommates—Timothy, Ned, and Oliver—deep into the desert lands of Arizona in search of the headquarters of the Brotherhood. Four individuals must present themselves as candidates—as a "Receptacle"—because one must die by his own hand, and a second must die at the hands of his companions so that two may gain immortality.

Although Barry N. Malzberg, surely one of Silverberg's most enthusiastic supporters, has declared that this is Silverberg's finest novel, he has also asserted that "not under any condition" can it be classified as science fiction. [2] His definition must be rigorous. Silverberg allows Eli to tell a girl whom he has picked up in a Manhattan bar that he is headed for Arizona; then Eli reflects, "Thank you, H. Rider Haggard; exactly." [3] Silverberg used the structure of the classical utopian tale as a framework for "A Happy Day in 2381"; similarly, except for the convention of the beautiful princess/priestess, he has infused the structure of the lost-race story into *The Book of Skulls*.

Once again Silverberg's technical know-how has given new vitality to traditional material. Yet he faced another problem, for the narrative perspective is an essential factor in this novel. No single point of view could encompass it. Silverberg thus chose to present the overlapping, fragmented interior monologues of the four youths participating in the quest: Eli, the Jewish intellectual from Manhattan; Oliver, the orphaned farm boy who has worked hard to escape from Kansas by gaining a full scholarship as a pre-med; Ned, the Catholic, Boston-Irish homosexual who would be an artist; Timothy, a member of the WASP aristocracy, who is bored with the whole idea and comes along for the ride.

Yet this manner of narration only signals the beginning of Silverberg's skill, for he has taken perhaps the most romantic myth/quest of the western imagination and fused it into contemporary, present-day America: here-and-now. Eli voices the central theme when he demands "a flight from reason" as "necessary." Demanding that his companions see "how hollow religion has become in the last hundred years," he insists that "Reason wasn't sufficient. Western man escaped from superstitious ignorance into materialistic emptiness." [4] The journey to find the "skull-house" in Arizona thus becomes a search by each of the four to "find that right thing, the synthesis," [5] to give spiritual substance to a universe which has been drained of meaning.

As is characteristic of the novels of the 1970's, action is reduced to a minimum in favor (especially during the first half of the narrative) of the outpourings of the youths who serve as an emblem of the whole of American society. Throughout the novel, both during the transit of the country and during their trial by the "Fraters" of the Brotherhood, much of their states of mind is presented in terms of sexual imagery and incident. Silverberg has been severely critized for the explicit sexuality of his later novels. However, what critics have apparently overlooked is a consistent pattern: sexuality—in all its variations—is used as a metaphor to convey important themes: the attempt (and often the failure) to communicate and, consequently, the superficiality and emptiness of human life that is isolated in the transient physical moment and knows nothing but its own tortured consciousness.

These outpourings are necessary so that the reader understands the reach of each young man to the training that they must undergo as a "group." The final act in their trial is that each must confess to one of the others: each "was going to become the custodian of someone else's secret . . . . The purge was what counted, the unburdening, rather than the information revealed." [6] Eli is the only one to break the seal of the confessional. Even less surprising, his sin is "an intellectual one, the most damning of all." [7] while those of the other three are sexual. At the end, although Eli finds himself "alone on a dark polar plateau, clawing at a universe whose gods had fled," he gives hiself "joyously, expectantly, undoubtingly . . . to the Skull and its Keepers." [8] It is a desperate gesture rising from his as yet unanswered needs. *The Book of Skulls* belongs, finally, to the dark side of Silverberg's fiction.

9. *Dying Inside* (1972)

In a sense, particularly when one considers the discrepancies and overlapping between probable dates of composition and dates of publication, Lissa Morgan of *The Second Trip* seems a kind of rehearsal for David Selig, the protagonist of *Dying Inside* (1972). Yet the centrality of Selig to Silverberg's imagination calls up other characters as well: most obviously, Hallinan of "Warm Man" in that Selig calls himself a "voyeur" [1]; Noel Vorst of *To Open the Sky* in that Vorst loses his precognitive powers; and, to some extent on a comic level, the adolescent protagonist of "Push No More" (1972), who simultaneously loses his virginity and his telekinetic power, sinking, as a result, "numbly into the quicksand, into the first moments of the long colorless years ahead." [2]

Although Silverberg received a special John W. Campbell award for his characterization of Selig, the general reaction of reviewers and critics was at best mixed, if not hostile. As late as 1977, it precipitated "the *Dying Inside* Debate" in *SF Commentary*, one of the most prestigious of the fanzines. In 1981 at the Modern Language Association meeting, Barry Malzberg declared that it was a "maintream," naturalistic novel and should not be categorized as science fiction. [3] Willis McNelly has called it a "most complex work . . . a Bildungsroman," in which "Life, Death, Rebirth . . . crowd the pages." [4]

Those who have dismissed Selig as the nastiest of anti-heroes again seem to have overlooked Silverberg's desire not only to study a character outside the main flow of everyday life but, more importantly, to use his experience at the metaphorical level. Certainly no more naturalistic than *The Book of Skulls*, *Dying Inside* permits David Selig to tell his own story. In New York City here-and-now he is a Jewish intellectual—nearly forty years old—who writes term papers for students at Columbia because he no longer believes that he can "make it" in the adult world. Since childhood he has had telepathic powers; yet essentially he can "only receive" and has "never had much conscious control over the ability." [5] He judges himself harshly—"the voyeur," as noted—and speaks of himself as "the miserable freakish fluke who can read the thoughts of others. Mutants, all of us. Genetic sports." [6] In short, he has been set apart through no fault of his own; moreover, from his childhood on, he has hidden the power. It frightens people; "wide open to everyone's innermost thoughts," he has become extremely vulnerable, growing "poor at giving love because he doesn't much trust his fellow humans." [7]

In a term paper that he writes on Kafka, Selig emphasizes that the theme running throughout Kafka's novels is "the impossibility of human communication." [8] This problem, so common to Silverberg's protagonists, lies at the heart of Selig's anguish. For now as he grows older, he finds that he is losing the ability. Though he has hated it because it separated him from others, it has also provided him with ecstasy, as when it allows him contact with creatures of the forest. It was for this "affirmation and fulfillment" that he had received "my blessing, my power." [9] Yet this experience is only momentarily satisfying, for it does not include humanity; once it vanishes, "how," he asks, "will you be able to touch them at all?" [10] He has felt keenly a "bitterness, [a] sour sense of isolation." [11] When the Black student, Yahya Lumamba, beats him up because the paper Selig wrote is unacceptable to the angry young Black, Selig is hospitalized, and the authorities at Columbia try briefly to help him, releasing him without pressing charges. Asked how he is, Selig replies that he is fine—"Except for the silence." [12]

Silverberg develops the narrative in three ways. First, he includes the texts of papers that Selig has written. Second, he allows Selig to speak of himself objectively as he reflects upon the meaning of his loss. Third and primarily, however, using flashbacks, Selig gives first-person accounts of his experience with various individuals, especially his mistress Toni and his sister Judith. Many of the incidents involve sexuality, for, as Selig rationalizes, "sex is, after all, a way of establishing communication with other human beings." [13] Basically the relationships are unsatisfactory; they either leave him or seem to fear him, though they do not harm him. At one point he cries out, "Entropy beats us down" and later in an essay cites Norbert Wiener's assertion that "as entropy increases, the universe, and all closed systems in the universe, tend naturally to deteriorate and lose their distinctiveness . . . ." [14] Although his telepathy has involved pain—"Who isn't in pain?" [15]—it has also given him his uniqueness. Without it, he loses his identity. As silence becomes his "mother tongue," Selig muses, "There will be discoveries and revelations, but no upheavals. Perhaps some color will come back into the world for me later. Perhaps." [16] At the end as he cries out, " . . . hello, hello, hello, hello," David Selig himself becomes Silverberg's most effective symbol of man's total isolation in an uncaring universe.

10. *The Stochastic Man* (1975)

In *Dying Inside* David Selig suggests that after the assassinations of Kennedy and King, after Czechoslovakia, Biafra, and Vietnam, "I knew there could be no hope for mankind . . . ." [1] *The Stochastic Man* (1975) extrapolates that feeling to the end of the century when New York City becomes the site of open guerilla warfare. In a sense it is the most political of Silverberg's fictions, for its protagonist, Lew Nicholls, is "obsessed with the idea of making Paul Quinn the President of the United States." [2] He helps him gain the mayorality of New York and begins to plan the maneuvers necessary to gain Quinn a presidential nomination in 2004.

Once again the novel is a first-person narrative told in retrospect so that its focus is on the state of Nicholls' mind. From the first page, the reader knows the outcome of the action, including the fact that Quinn both hates and fears Nicholls as a symbol of determinism. Thus the novel really becomes an exercise in philosophical speculation, opening with Nicholls' assertion, "We are born by accident into a purely random universe . . . . we swim each day through seas of chaos, and nothing is predictable, not even the events of the very next instant . . . . If you [believe that] I pity you, because yours must be a bleak and terrifying and comfortless life." [3] The entire narrative attempts to refute that view, for Nicholls is an expert in the field of probability.

The science-fiction "furniture" is reduced to a minimum: Nicholls comes under the influence of Martin Carvajal, an older man who "sees" into the future (at the time of the story his limit is seventeen months because at the end of that period he will be murdered while Nicholls looks on). Carvajal feeds Nicholls information in cryptic memos and informs him that "There's only one way for things to happen. You have no choice but to say and do the things I *saw* you say and do." [4] Again, "the future's immutable. We're both actors in a script that can't be rewritten." [5] He explains that in the past circumstances have always prevented him from changing any event he foresaw. Although Nicholls protests "Carvajal's unbending determinism" and rails against the "conservation of reality," [6] he voices his desire to be able to see into the future.

"Everyone has the gift," Carvajal explains. "Very few know how to use it." [7] Nicholls surrenders himself, allowing Carvajal to dictate the details of his life—from shaving his head to obtaining a divorce from the beautiful Sundara, whose family came from India. (Sundara becomes a follower of the Transit Creed, essentially a woman's movement; Silverberg does not use it as a vehicle of satire but rather as another means of exploring the issue of individual freedom.) Because Nicholls can only deliver his memos and cannot explain them, he comes under pressure and finally is fired by Quinn. While at Big Sur, Nicholls had the first of his visions. He saw Quinn as a dictator, comparing the scene explicitly to Hitler in 1934. [8] Later he learns that Quinn thinks of him as an "Antichrist."

Yet Silverberg does not replace randomness with inflexible determinism. When Nicholls tells Carvajal that he has seen many visions of his own death and cannot be certain which one is right, Carvajal replies simply, "There are many levels of reality." [9] After his death, Nicholls, as his heir, obtains the funds necessary to found the Center for Stochastic Processes.

The significance of *The Stochastic Man* is that it opens a new direction for Silverberg's speculations. As he rejects randomness, so he rejects determinism because it is too simple; "it doesn't have all the answers." [10] Through Lew Nicholls he is searching for a way in which man can learn and accept the future. In a final passage he refers to Jesus and Isis as having foreknowledge. Nicholls asserts that he has "come through the time of doubt" but has not fallen into "a paralysis such as afflicted Carvajal." Instead he dreams of the day when "We shall be as gods, all of us . . . . We will live in beauty, knowing that we are aspects of one great Plan." [11] Indefinite, vague, uncertain: yes, but Silverberg has come a long way from the depths of Selig's anguish. Perhaps more importantly, he has abandoned the transcendentalism of Gundersen and Tomis to find a new way of achieving his dream.

11. *Shadrach in the Furnace* (1976)

Silverberg published *Shadrach in the Furnace* (1976) a year after he had announced his retirement from the field and had ceased writing new fiction. Although it concerns itself with the events of the near future (2012) and expresses his pessimism about the political future of the world, it abandons the self-tortured protagonists of the last decade in favor of Shadrach Mordecai, personal physician to Genghis II Mao IV Khan, Prince of Princes, Chairman of Chairmen, and, obviously, ruler of the world.

Numerous receptor nodes have been implanted into Shadrach's body so that he constantly receives data regarding the bodily processes of the ninety-two-year-old Khan, who is already "a patchwork of artificial and transplanted organs" and thus remains "as strong and responsive as a man of fifty." [1] Basically Shadrach remains within signal range of the Khan, for, like a computer, his function is "to monitor, evaluate, and report on the moment-to-moment physiological changes within Genghis Mao's body." [2] The Chairman wishes "to postpone death until his work on earth is complete—which is to say, never to die," although Shadrach suspects that he must be "death-haunted, death-obsessed" to rule the world he has inherited by default. [3]

Through drugs administered by a "transtemporalist," Shadrach is able to travel back in time to August 19, 1991, the date of the catastrophe which so drastically changed the world. He witnesses the eruption of Cotopaxi overlooking Quito, Ecuador; " . . . there will be an explosion that will be heard thousands of miles away [even in Philadelphia by fifteen-year-old Shadrach Mordecai as he dreams of med school], the earthquake, the clouds of poisonous gas, the lunatic outpouring of tons of volcanic ash, and on the night of Cotopaxi the ancient gods will be let loose on earth and empires will crumple." [4] Beginning in Brazil, the eruption sets in motion a chain reaction of revolutions that sweep the globe. Were this not enough, there follows a terrible virus war whose end effect is to produce "organ-rot . . . the great medical phenomenon of the age, the latter-day Black Death, the most terrible epidemic in history." [5] Ironically, an antidote exists, but the Khan has not put it into "widespread distribution" because there is not enough to go around. Moreover, a "mad world which destroys itself with cloud-borne antigens" perhaps deserves only "hope not injections." [6] And so the ravaged people of a ruined earth suffer "lingering deaths." The virus "was capable of integrating into the nucleic acid, into the germ plasm itself, becoming so intimately entwined with the human genetic machinery" that, passing from generation to generation, it could seize an individual at any time. [7]

Knowing that Shadrach daily watches the television satellites so tht he may see "the rotting people all over the world," the Khan judges Shadrach to be *"a man of compassion. Childlike. Not saintly . . . . he thinks only of healing people. He would heal those who enslaved his ancestors even."* [8] The dramatic conflict arises because of "Project Avatar," whose aim is "to develop a personality-transfer technique" allowing the Khan "to move to a younger body." [9] When the political heir apparent learns that he has been chosen to donate his body to this worthy cause, he commits suicide. Shadrach learns that he has been selected as replacement. He asks to leave the capital for a time.

Silverberg structures the novel around three operations. The first, the Khan's third liver transplant within seven years, provides a convenient means of setting up characters and background. Shadrach performs the second, an abdominal aorta transplant to halt the threat of an aneurysm, after he has been told that he is to be the donor. During his journey into the suffering world, he declare that "organ-rot can be defeated," and in Jerusalem he asks the Lord to show him "how I can make [the world] more like the place you meant it to be." [10]

Once back in the capital, he finds Genghis II Mao IV the victim of severe headaches caused by intracranial pressure resulting from the accumulation of cerebrospinal fluid. During the third operation he inserts a valve to drain away the fluid, but at the same time he places a "piezoelectric crystal" into the palm of his hand so that he can control, even reverse, the action of the valve in the Chairman's skull. During the Khan's convalescence, Shadrach allows himself to experience once more the dream-death, during which he rises above time and space and sees himself as "the Healer," tending even Christ and Osiris. [11] Later he demonstrates his power to the Khan; when questioned he says that he will kill only in self defense. He asks only that as a member of the Committee he be given "authority" in the field of public health so that he may try to cure the organ-rot. The Khan, laughing, hails him as Genghis III, Mao V.

Silverberg has kept his focus upon Shadrach from the outset of the narrative. He has controlled Shadrach's idealism by implying that any transcendental experience may have been dream rather than reality. On the other hand, he has abandoned the underworld of despair. The distinction of *Shadrach in the Furnace* is that its protagonist makes an affirmative answer so that he himself may shape the world in which he lives.

NOTES

1. *Nightwings* (1969)

1. Silverberg, "Sounding Brass, Tinkling Cymbal," p. 35.
2. Ibid., p. 39.
3. Brian W. Stableford, "Nightwings," in *Survey of Science Fiction Literature*, ed. Frank N. Magill (Englewood Cliffs, N.J.: Salem Press, 1979), III, 1528, 1529.
4. Stableford, III, 1529.
5. Silverberg, *Nightwings* (New York: Avon Equinox Edition, 1976), p. 96.
6. Ibid., p. 97.
7. Ibid., pp. 42, 43.
8. Ibid., pp. 71, 41.
9. Ibid., p. 37.
10. Ibid., p. 60.
11. Ibid., pp. 33, 103.
12. Ibid. pp. 98, 99, 100.
13. Ibid., pp. 102, 103.

14. Ibid., pp. 113-114.
15. Ibid., pp. 114, 145.
16. Ibid., pp. 186-187.

2. *Downward to the Earth* (1970)

1. Silverberg, "Introduction," *A Robert Silverberg Omnibus* (New York: Harper & Row, 1981), pp. ix, x.
2. Clareson, "Downward to the Earth," in *Survey of Science Fiction Literature*, ed. Frank N. Magill, II, 592.
3. Silverberg, *Downward to the Earth* (Garden City, N.Y.: Nelson Doubleday, Inc., 1970), p. 15.
4. Ibid., p. 116
5. Clareson, II, 593.
6. Silverberg, *Downward to the Earth*, pp. 116, 118.
7. Clareson, "The Fictions of Robert Silverberg," *Voices for the Future*, II, 20.
8. Silverberg, *Downward to the Earth*, p. 166.
9. Ibid., p. 178.
10. H. W. Hall, *Science Fiction Book Review Index, 1923-1973*, pp. 280-281. See also my *Robert Silverberg: A Primary and Secondary Bibliography*, to be published by G. K. Hall in 1983.

3. *Tower of Glass* (1970)

1. Silverberg, "Sounding Brass, Tinkling Cymbal," p. 40.
2. James Gunn, "Tower of Glass," in *Survey of Science Fiction Literature*, ed. Frank N. Magill, V, 2303-2305.
3. I asked Gunn this question at the SFRA meeting in Lawrence, Kansas, in July, 1982. I mention his reply here, but I do not wish to do him any injustice; in the midst of the Conference, we did not have an opportunity to discuss the problem at length.
4. Silverberg, *Tower of Glass* (New York: Bantam Books, 1971), pp. 40-41.
5. Ibid., pp. 95-96.
6. Ibid., p. 96.
7. Ibid., p. 135.
8. Ibid., pp. 19-20.
9. Ibid., pp. 11, 13.
10. Ibid., pp. 10, 136.
11. Ibid., p. 4.
12. Ibid., p. 70.
13. Ibid., p. 80.
14. Ibid., p. 159.
15. Ibid., p. 169.
16. Ibid., p. 184.
17. Clareson, "The Fictions of Robert Silverberg," II, 30.

4. *A Time of Changes* (1971)

1. Brian W. Stableford, "A Time of Changes," in *Survey of Science Fiction Literature*, ed. Frank N. Magill, V, 2293-2297.
2. Silverberg, "Introduction," *A Time of Changes* (New York: Berkley, 1979), pp. viii, ix.
3. Silverberg, *A Time of Changes*, pp. 21, 26, 27.
4. Ibid., pp. 97, 98.
5. Ibid., pp. 106, 99.
6. Ibid., p. 157.
7. Ibid., p. 214.
8. Silverberg, "Introduction," *A Time of Changes*, p. x.

5. *Son of Man* (1971)

1. Silverberg, "Sounding Brass, Tinkling Cymbal," p. 39.
2. Brian Stableford, "Reviews of *The Second Trip* and *Son of Man*," *Vector #96* (December 1979/January 1980), p. 39.
3. Silverberg, *Son of Man* (New York: Ballantine Books, 1971), pp. 8, 9.
4. Ibid., p. 20.
5. Ibid., pp. 35, 37.
6. Ibid., pp. 45-52.
7. Ibid., pp. 190-191, 210-211.

6. *The World Inside* (1971)

1. Silverberg, "untitled headnote," *The Best of Robert Silverberg* (Boston: Gregg Press, 1978), II, 1.
2. Silverberg, "Sounding Brass, Tinkling Cymbal," p. 40.
3. Silverberg, *The World Inside* (New York: New American Library, 1971), p. 18.
4. Ibid., p. 19.
5. Ibid., p. 14.
6. Ibid., p. 18.
7. Ibid., p. 15.
8. Ibid., p. 11.
9. Ibid., pp. 11-12.
10. Ibid., pp. 19-20.
11. Ibid., p. 21.

7. *The Second Trip* (1972)

1. Silverberg, "Sounding Brass, Tinkling Cymbal," p. 41.
2. Ibid., p. 40.
3. Silverberg, *The Second Trip* (New York: Nelson Doubleday,

1972), pp. 87, 185.
4. Ibid., p. 124.
5. Ibid., p. 128.

8. *The Book of Skulls* (1972)

1. Silverberg, *Recalled to Life* (New York: Doubleday, 1972), pp. 183-184.
2. Barry Malzberg, "Robert Silverberg," *F&SF*, 46 (April 1974), p. 71.
3. Silverberg, *The Book of Skulls* (New York: Scribners, 1972), 25
4. Ibid., p. 57.
5. Ibid., p. 57.
6. Ibid., p. 170.
7. Ibid., p. 203.
8. Ibid., p. 221.

9. *Dying Inside* (1972)

1. Silverberg, *Dying Inside* (New York: Scribners, 1972), p. 17.
2. Silverberg, "Push No More," *Unfamiliar Territory* (New York: Scribners, 1973), p. 132.
3. Tape recording of a dialogue between Barry Malzberg and Thomas D. Clareson, dated 29 December 1981.
4. Willis McNelly, "*Dying Inside*," in *Survey of Science Fiction Literature*, ed. Frank N. Magill, II, 673.
5. Silverberg, *Dying Inside*, p. 17.
6. Ibid., pp. 26-27.
7. Ibid., p. 52.
8. Ibid., p. 22.
9. Ibid., pp. 228, 229.
10. Ibid., p. 30.
11. Ibid., p. 75.
12. Ibid., p. 231.
13. Ibid., p. 140.
14. Ibid., pp. 82, 203.
15. Ibid., p. 91.
16. Ibid., p. 245.

10. *The Stochastic Man* (1975)

1. Silverberg, *Dying Inside*, p. 51.
2. Silverberg, *The Stochastic Man* (New York: Harper & Row, 1975), p. 17.
3. Ibid., p. 5.
4. Ibid., p. 93.
5. Ibid., p. 93.

6. Ibid., p. 201.
7. Ibid., p. 137.
8. Ibid., pp. 188-189.
9. Ibid., p. 234.
10. Ibid., p. 9.
11. Ibid., p. 240.

11. *Shadrach in the Furnace* (1976)

1. Silverberg, *Shadrach in the Furnace* (Indianapolis, IN: Bobbs-Merrill, 1976), p. 2.
2. Ibid., p. 24.
3. Ibid., p. 17.
4. Ibid., p. 42.
5. Ibid., p. 181.
6. Ibid., p. 176.
7. Ibid., p. 185.
8. Ibid., p. 133.
9. Ibid., p. 20.
10. Ibid., p. 198.
11. Ibid., p. 239.

V

THE SHORTER FICTION: 1969 - 1974

Any discussion of Silverberg's later short fiction must begin with "Sundance," which he wrote in September, 1968, [1] although it was not published until the following June. Certainly one of his most successful technical achievements, it may well have initiated that period when he deliberately experimented in an effort to bring science fiction closer to what innovative writers were then doing in "mainstream" fiction. Its point of departure is one familiar to the field: to ready an unnamed planet for terran colonists, a team is exterminating the herds of a dominant animal, the so-called "Eaters." The central complication occurs when the man Herndon casually asks how his partner would react if they discovered that the supposed pests were, indeed, intelligent beings: "people."

Silverberg made two crucial decisions. First, Herndon's partner is the Sioux Indian, Tom Two Ribbons. Although he has "not yet found his own mode of self-destruction," he has suffered a breakdown and has been subjected to a "personality reconstruct." His racial inheritance ensures that he will brood over Herndon's idle speculation. Granted, then, that Tom Two Ribbons must be the protagonist, the second decision must make certain that the narrative perspective develops the story's full potential. If told completely in the first person, Tom could easily become no more than another suffering individual; the story, no more than another tale of social protest, a distinct possibility since Silverberg develops the analogy between the Eaters and both the American bison and the Sioux: animal or human?

Because Silverberg must focus on Tom, he employs three perspectives to develop fully the ambiguities of the dilemma. Beginning with the first sentence, the second-person—"Today you liquidated about 50,000 Eaters in Sector A"—directly involves the reader in the emotion of the situation. Through the first person, one watches Tom dance with the creatures and eat with them the oxygen-liberating plants which may have, especially for humans, an hallucogenic effect; one listens to him identify the Eaters with his ancestors. Through the third person, not only does one see Tom objectively as he walks among "a straggling herd, nibbling delicately . . ." but one also listens to his companions suggest that the entire affair is part of Tom's therapy intended to exorcise his racial paranoia. (One must also judge the society which would use such therapy.) Tom loses all sense of reality. With him, "you"—the reader—fall through, oscillating from one idea to another; total ambiguity. Yet content and form have been fused.

As Silverberg has pointed out, during these years "the stories show a preoccupation with technique," and he acknowledges his indebtedness to such writers as Donald Barthelme, Jorge Luis Borges, and Robert Coover. [2] In a number of narratives he displays a humor largely absent from his novels. "(Now + n) (Now - n)" (1972) recounts the love story of a man who has contact with himself in the near future (+ n) and the near past (-n). Thus he has great success on the stock market and with a woman who cannot stabilize her place in the time-stream without the aid of an amulet given her by an admirer while she was in the twenty-fifth century. Of course her amulet negates his psi power. As noted elsewhere, [3] building upon the idea of murdering one's spouse, the delightful "Many Mansions" (1973) combines all of the time-travel paradoxes, handling them in a fragmented narrative which recalls Coover's "Babysitter" in that by its end one does not know who has done what to whom. In "How It Was When the Past Went Away," he plays with the idea of someone's dumping amnisifacient drugs into the water supply of San Francisco. Yet something in his pervasive dissatisfaction compels him to end the story on the note that from the experience a new religion has emerged: "maybe a cult that offered emancipation from all inner burdens." [4] The humor vanishes.

"In the Group" (1973) deals with the shockingly anti-social behavior of young Murray, who desires a one-to-one relationship with Kay instead of sharing her, with the aid of a machine enabling telepathic unity, in group sex. Again the humor evaporates, however, as Murray, dismissed from the group, wanders aimlessly through the world, looking for he knows not what.

Silverberg has called some of the stories from this period parodies of science fiction [5]; among them are "Good News from the Vatican" (1971), which won him a Nebula, and "Caliban" (1971). Until its surprise ending, the former is little more than a dialogue among tourists awaiting the white smoke signifying that a robot has been elected Pope. "Caliban" is more substantial and more deceptive, for its parody rises out of Silverberg's manipulation of the traditional science fiction encounter between present-day man and the citizens of a seemingly paradisicial world. The principal accomplishment of the advanced, "sweet Aryanized world" seems to have been reached through genetic engineering.

Everyone is a blue-eyed blonde, having a trim, athletic torso. Caliban begins his narrative by telling the reader that the people "have all changed their faces to a standard model . . . the latest thing." He himself is the latest "Thing," the current diversion amidst aimless leisure. His chief activity is to copulate with a variety of identical women whose names he must ask so as not to call them by the wrong name. The women apparently must take an aphrodisiac before coupling with him. The tone is sharpened when authorities inform him that he is the "sole representative of the nightmare out of which we have awakened." [6] Forced to breathe water, Caliban asserts that the ability to do so must come from "genetic modification." His companion laughs, urging him to "think more positively about this business . . . . Don't you realize that it's a major evolutionary step . . . . Don't you want to be part of the great leap forward?" [7] Silverberg explains nothing; through Caliban, he simply confronts the reader with the situation.

One also cannot be sure whether or not Silverberg is able in this story to parody the theme of alienation. Caliban insists that he must be transformed. Although he believes that he occasionally sees someone who resembles him (he thinks such persons must have been brought to this time period), when he awakens, he finds that the beautiful citizens have assumed his grotesque form as the newest model. "How I despise them!" he concludes. "I am the only golden one. And all of them mocking me by their metamorphosis." [8]

The same ennui apparent in the society of "Caliban" grips the contemporary suburbanites of "When We Went to See the End of the World" (1970). The couples treat this latest fad in tourism casually; what could be a unifying apocalyptic experience becomes instead a source of bickering and jealousy because it is not the same for any two couples. The reports of catastrophes fed them by the media have deadened their sensibilities; they do not realize that they are spiritually dead and that their present-day society has already been destroyed because of their indifference to major issues. Therein lies the irony of the story. The suggestion that one scene relies heavily on H. G. Wells' *The Time Machine* has been strengthened by the cover illustration for the paperback edition of *Unfamiliar Territory*. [9] One suspects that Silverberg has drawn upon numerous earlier science-fiction stories for the scenes depicting the end of the world, for his works from this period, whether novel or shorter fiction, are widely and richly allusive.

As well as fragmenting the narrative, as he does often in stories from the 1970's, Silverberg has followed his contemporaries' use of another convention to convey a sense of ambiguity and disorder. Either in the guise of a character stepping back from the narrative or in a direct intrusion speaking in his own voice, the writer reminds the reader that fiction is an artificial construct rather than a piece of reality. In "Some Notes on the Pre-Dynastic Epoch" (1973), using the first-person, a "Metalinguistic Archaeologist, Third Grade" at some unspecified time in the future describes the artifacts that have come to him from his beloved twentieth century, as well as recounting how he and two companions passed through "a gate of dreams" so that they could enter the ruined past. Early in the story, however, he abruptly announces, "None of the aforegoing is true. I take pleasure in deceiving. I am an extremely unreliable witness." [10] Later, after he laments the collapse of twentieth-century civilization, during which he has included newspaper clippings, a list of topics requiring further analysis, and the judgment from the Book of Daniel ["Mene, Mene, Tekel, Upharsin"], he confesses, "I am your contemporary. I am your brother. These notes are the work of a pre-dynastic man like yourself, a native of the so-called Twentieth Century, who, like you, has lived through dark hours and may live to see darker ones . . . . Do I seem reliable now? Can you trust me, just this once?" [11]

In "Ms. Found in an Abandoned Time Machine" (1973) Silverberg introduces "Thomas C_____, our chief protagonist," a militant young idealist. The narrative mixes together incidents that could be reported by the media and such events from Thomas' career as saving Lincoln from assassination so that, perhaps, the racial problem will be solved. At one point Thomas asserts that "reader and writer have to be allies, co-conspirators." Again, "It's all done with the aid of a lot of science fiction gadgetry. I won't apologize for that part of it." [12] He claims that he is a traveler from the far future visiting the year 1972. After he has zapped the current president ("Dick") in order to blow his mind so that he carries out needed reforms, Thomas breaks down: "Oh. Oh. Oh. Oh, God. If it could only be that easy. One, two, three, zap . . . . How was I able to trick you into a suspension of disbelief? . . . I'm a bunch of symbols on a piece of paper. I'm just something abstract trapped within a mere fiction." [13] The final irony occurs when Thomas is killed by the very audience which he has called to action.

Thomas' reference to "science fiction gadgetry" leads one to "The Science Fiction Hall of Fame" (1973), in which Silverberg juxtaposes many of the clichéd scenes from traditional science fiction with the admission of the narrator that he is too deeply involved in such fantasies. He even addresses the difficulty of considering science fiction "adult literature" because it deals "with unreal situations set in places that do not exist in eras that have not yet occurred." [14] Despite his apprehensions, however, the narrator uses science fiction as an escape, as it launches him on a journey permitting him to avoid the mundane world and its human responsibilities.

In contrast to the emotional outbursts of such stories is the melancholic tone of the narrator of "The Wind and the Rain" (1973), the spokesman of a reclamation team that comes to Earth to restore the ruined planet. When he and his companions enter the last human refuge in Uruguay, finding its small population mummified, he admits, "I am moved almost to tears, as are several of the others." [15] Only then does the reader learn that the team are descendants of persons who fled the Earth before its final downfall. A change in tone occurs when they find a robot on the Tibetan plateau; they are "favorably impressed by the durability and resilience of these machines. Perhaps in the distant future such entities will wholly replace the softer and more fragile life-forms on all worlds, as they seem to have done on Earth." [16]

Trying to find a meaningful pattern within Silverberg's shorter fiction, one is impressed by his variety and versatility. His work ranges from "Black Is Beautiful" (1970), in which he captures the Black anger but includes their rationalizations perpetuating their segregation in cities, like New York, which they control, to the comic "Something Wild Is Loose" (1971), in which the alien Vsiir arranges to go home only after he enters the mind of a woman in a coma and communicates with the neuropathologist who is treating her. Silverberg employs the same situation in "A Sea of Faces" (1974) to dramatize the entrapment of a doctor in the disordered mind of his patient during a "consciousness-penetrating" treatment.

The stories range from "The Feast of St. Dionysus" (1973), the ambiguous and mystical tale of Oxenshuer, the sole survivor of the first NASA flight to Mars, to "Thomas the Proclaimer" (1972), the account of the world's rejection of a direct sign from God. In a way the latter seems a pessimistic rewriting of *The Masks of Time*, for Thomas is killed and irrationality reigns.

At the center of all the short stories stands "In Entropy's Jaws" (1970), which Silverberg has judged the "most challenging of all my time stories." [17] It focuses upon John Skein, who is able to fuse minds together so that individuals may work out business deals without knowing the entirety of one another because Skein controls them. One such contact burns Skein out. Thereafter he experiences "time fugues"—temporal disorientation which blacks him out and send him randomly along the time-line. Only on Abbondanza IV, after he merges with an amoeba-like creature, does he seem to escape "the illusion of linearity." [18] He finds, however, that he has trapped himself in a cyclic action, for he understands that he himself is the old man on Abbondanza who aided him. Silverberg uses the story as a framework for a discussion of entropic effect, randomness, and determinism. The same concerns infuse "Trips" (1973), a deceptively simple story involving the narrator's restless (and endless?) quest among parallel worlds. In contrast, although the concept of entropy is also essential to "What We learned from This Morning's Newspaper" (1972), the effect of that story differs radically. Its storyline makes use of the old science-fiction gimmick of getting tomorrow's newspaper early (in this case the *New York Times* for December 1 on November 22). The first-person narrator gives a straightforward account of how he and his fortunate neighbors on Redbud Crescent plan to use the information to make a financial killing. During the week they notice that the print of the paper fades, and one of them mentions "entropic creep." On December 1 they receive the paper for November 22, but the news is drastically different. They emerge from their homes to find the world shrouded in a "gray like a thick fog"—which makes one think of the climax of Jerome Bixby's classic "It's a *Good* Life." Thus Silverberg transforms a seeming parody into a horror story.

"Caught in the Organ Draft" (1972) is also something of a horror story, although its tone is predominantly bitter. Wars and such nonsense have been done away with because the older generation needs the youth to supply it with organ transplants. The narrator, like all of his nineteen-year-old contemporaries, must sign up for the draft and report to Transplant House for examination. Although he debates evading the draft, he surrenders a kidney when called to service. With that act, his loyalty shifts. In the future he will take all of the organs that he possibly can.

The finest short work of the period may well be "Breckenridge and the Continuum" (1972), although Silverberg has called it "not so much a story . . . as a series of terrifying vignettes." [19] In it he plays with content as he deliberately garbles the classical myths and with literary criticism as he introduces "some possible structural hypotheses" and a "hypothesis of structural resolution" to lead his readers ambiguously to the narrative's various levels of meaning. Against the familiar assertion regarding "the meaninglessness of life . . . empty, dumb, mechanical," Noel Breckenridge alternates between the contemporary scene and "an unimaginably altered world at the end of time" in which he searches for an unnamed city. In that world he is instructed to relate the myths and legends which he had learned in his childhood, although one of his listeners remarks contemptuously that he has heard these tales in countless forms. "Gradually the outlines of a master myth took place . . . the coming of a redeemer to start the cycle anew." [20] Just as it seems that Breckenridge may be that redeemer, answering the riddle given Oedipus so that the builders of the city, lying in suspended animation, may awaken and begin life anew, the world vanishes. Yet Breckenridge disappears into the Sahara, "very very happy" in his quest, although it seems to have no effect upon the events taking place in the world. Certainly "Breckenridge and the Continuum" remains one of his most complex and ambitious works.

Before he turned to *The Stochastic Man* and *Shadrach in the Furnace*, Silverberg wrote what he has regarded as one last important short story, "Schwartz Between the Galaxies" (1974) for Judy-Lynn del Rey. [21] A famous anthropologist on a lecture tour, Schwartz despises "the one huge sophisticated plastic western state" that engulfs the world. Since he believes that man is isolated in a barren solar system and is incapable of reaching the stars, he fantasizes. He imagines himself on an intergalactic voyage with numerous aliens as his companions. (Silverberg alternates scenes between the world tour which is killing Schwartz and the idealized scenes in which he communicates happily with the aliens.) Ironically, even in his fantasy, he cannot rid himself of the Yale economist, Pitkin, who has no imagination. On the world-tour the Stewardess Dawn is more available than sympathetic. Only aboard the starship does he have a sense of belonging—of unity—"perhaps attainable only through death." [22]

If one examines "Born with the Dead" (1974), the novella which won him a Nebula, one learns that death is not a satisfactory answer. Its storyline focuses upon the efforts of Jorge Klein to communicate with Sybille, his wife, who has undergone the process of "rekindling" after she died. He will not give up his pursuit of her, though he is constantly rejected both by her and by her companions. He follows them from Zanzibar to one of the cities of the "Deads" in Utah. At one point he imagines a conversation with her in which she declares " . . . Everything is quiet where I am . . . . There's a peace that passeth all understanding." [23] This provides the key to the story's irony. Her companions poison Klein. On the third day after his own "rekindling," Sybille and her friends come to him, filled with plans for their amusement during the coming winter. He realizes then that "they cavort emotionlessly in a meaningless life-in-death" [24] despite their continuous activities. Through their fear of death, they have chosen an empty immortality made up of trifling details. Yet because Klein chose Sybille and thus death, he has become one of them, although he feels that he has no need of them and does not join their "set." Nevertheless, although he does not see Sybille again for years, in a vivid concluding image, " . . . they spent the last days of '99 together, shooting dodos under the shadow of mighty Kilimanjaro." [25]

Ignoring his novels for the moment, one must realize that during the 1970's no other science-fiction writer did as much as Silverberg to prove that science fiction can serve effectively not only as a vehicle for entertainment and social protest, but, more importantly, as a means for creating new metaphors to illuminate the condition of modern man. (This ability did not suddenly appear from nowhere in the 1970's; in the just-released *World of a Thousand Colors* (1982), containing nineteen stories written between 1957 and 1971, one can sense Silverberg's desire to experiment with traditional materials.) One does not wish to speculate how closely his thematic concerns reflected his personal feelings, but one must note that his often convoluted narratives and his tortured protagonists caught much of the essence of despair that shaped the American scene during the period.

NOTES

1. Silverberg, "untitled headnote," *The Best of Robert Silverberg*, I, 227.
2. Silverberg, "Introduction," *Unfamiliar Territory* (New York: Berkley, 1978), pp. x, xi.
3. Clareson, "The Fictions of Robert Silverberg," II, 3.
4. Silverberg, "How It Was When the Past Went Away," *World of a Thousand Colors* (New York: Arbor House, 1982), p. 329.
5. Silverberg, "Sounding Brass, Tinkling Cymbal," p. 41.
6. Silverberg, "Caliban," *Unfamiliar Territory*, p. 64.
7. Ibid., p. 67.
8. Ibid., p. 74.
9. This is the Berkley edition already cited. The cover shows the red sun and a crab-like creature; in a 'crystal' ball, a couple obviously on a picnic watch the scene.
10. Silverberg, "Some Notes on the Pre-Dynastic Epoch," *Unfamiliar Territory*, p. 36.
11. Ibid., p. 44.
12. Silverberg, "Ms. Found in an Abandoned Time Machine," *Capricorn Games* (New York: Random House, 1976), pp. 41, 51.
13. Ibid., p. 54.
14. Silverberg, "The Science Fiction Hall of Fame," *Capricorn Games*, p. 29.
15. Silverberg, "The Wind and the Rain," *Unfamiliar Territory*, p. 204.
16. Ibid., p. 207.
17. Silverberg, "untitled headnote," *The Best of Robert Silverberg*, II, 21.
18. Silverberg, "In Entropy's Jaws," *Unfamiliar Territory*, p. 172.
19. Silverberg, "untitled headnote," *The Best of Robert Silverberg*, II, 119.
20. Silverberg, "Breckenridge and the Continuum," *Capricorn*

Games, p. 80.

21. Silverberg, "untitled headnote," *The Best of Robert Silverberg*, II, 299.

22. Clareson, "The Fictions of Robert Silverberg," II, 12.

23. Silverberg, "Born with the Dead," *Born with the Dead* (New York: Vintage Books, 1975), p. 73.

24. Clareson, "The Fictions of Robert Silverberg," II, 27.

25. Silverberg, *Born with the Dead*, p. 97.

VI

MAJIPOOR (1980 -)

One must realize that although Silverberg did not produce any new fiction for something like four years after the spring of 1975, he did not abandon science fiction. He edited a number of anthologies, he wrote introductions to new editions of many of his works, and he did some reviewing. One column, "Opinions," which began in *Galileo*, has become a feature of *Amazing/ Fantastic*. By 1979, however, it was generally known that he was working on a new novel.

One does not know to what degree *Lord Valentine's Castle* (1980)—serialized in *F&SF* during the autumn and winter of 1979-1980—caught his audience by surprise, although it did gain Nebula and Hugo nominations. It was not political, nor did it advocate the need for social change. Its protagonist did not suffer nor seek redemption in a meaningless universe. Nor did he indulge in an explicitly described sexual liaison.

One wonders to what extent Silverberg had been consciously influenced by the ascendancy of fantasy in the late 1970's. For *Lord Valentine's Castle* dramatizes an heroic quest. As its point of departure, Silverberg employs a convention long familiar to the field: the enemies of the protagonist transfer his mind to a different body to deprive him of political power, for he is the Coronal of the planet Majipoor. Alone and amnesiac, the youthful Valentine ventures into the ancient city of Pidruid, where he joins a troupe of entertainers led by Zalzan Kavol, learning to become a juggler. Under this guise, unconsciously at first, he will attempt to regain his title. From the outset Valentine can be identified as a traditional heir; as noted elsewhere, he personifies the mythic lost heir without whom "the mainstream of British fiction could not have survived, perhaps even in this century." [1] When the beautiful young woman whom he loves, Carabella, dreams that he is Coronal Lord Valentine, he initially scoffs at the suggestion, insisting that he is no more than a wandering juggler. Yet once planted—and reinforced by his own dreams as well as the aid of a mystic dwarf and a fortune teller—the idea is accepted. Soon he speculates about the problem of governing well in a manner recalling King Arthur and Shakespeare's Henry V as they think on the qualities of an ideal king. [2] Later Valentine asserts " . . . let it not be said of Lord Valentine that he regained his throne with magnificent heroism and then ruled feebly and aimlessly for fifty years." [3] No reader can doubt that he will fulfill his quest, but before he does, there remains much to see and do.

Nobody can deny that the storyline is traditional and, perhaps, somewhat thin, but to acknowledge this is not to criticize Silverberg. His essential strategy becomes apparent as soon as he permits Valentine to join the wandering jugglers. In creating Majipoor, Silverberg has conjured up an exotic world surpassing even those of Herbert's *Dune* and LeGuin's *The Left Hand of Darkness*—not in terms of ingenuity and vividness, but rather in terms of its vastness and the opportunity for a wide variety of adventures. In short, Valentine's assumed identity allows Silverberg to open up the panorama of Majipoor, which was settled some fourteen thousand years ago by human and then by a number of alien races—the Skandars, the Vroons, the Ghayrogs—at the invitation of its human rulers. Nor should one forget its first people, the Metamorphs—the feared Shapechangers—who still pose a threat though ancient wars almost exterminated them. Since Majipoor does not lie astride the main trade routes of the galaxy, it has been left to itself. So vast is the planet that its Great Sea has not yet been crossed; its continents have not been fully explored and settled. At first impression, especially because of the emphais both upon physical prowess and upon its wilderness, it seems a barbaric world whose civilization has tumbled from some golden age. Not until the last struggle for Castle Mount, the home of the Coronal, does the reader learn that ancient weather machines "create an eternal springtime" atop the mountain which extends into the stratosphere. [4]

Thus Valentine's quest and assumed identity allow Silverberg to structure his narrative episodically, each sequence largely self-contained and separate, although, of course, all trace Valentine's journey from Pidruid to his throne. Moreover, the incidents call up innumerable literary echoes. Valentine may flee down the River Steiche to escape from the horrors of the province of the Metamorphs rather than to undertake a Conradian journey into the interior, but it makes the reader remember Silverberg's earlier use of Conrad. That the tone of *Lord Valentine's Castle* differs radically from his earlier novels, as well as from Conrad, may be seen in his emphasis upon external incident. The rafts are wrecked and the companions separated and reunited within a single chapter so that Silverberg may get on to something else. When Valentine and his companions go as pilgrims to The Isle of Dreams to seek the Lady of the Isle so that she may identify Valentine as her son and the true Coronal, the names and tone of the incident call up the Arthurian legend.

Nor can Silverberg's humor be overlooked. In Lisamon Hultin, "who hires as bodyguard and warrior," [5] Silverberg has created one of the delightfully comic and memorable Amazons of science fiction. She figures importantly throughout the novel, especially in one of the sequences that illustrates Silverberg's ability to adapt literary sources to his own ends. Valentine's friends embark on the ill-fated ship, *Brangalyn*, whose captain allows them aboard so long as they do not interfere with his dragon-hunting. When Lord Kinniken's dragon—famous for its "vast and implausible bulk"—rams and sinks the ship, "who does not think of Moby Dick?" At that point Silverberg asserts his individuality, "for few scenes can parody heroic adventure (and thus in this instance parody one's own deliberate, carefully manipulted actions) more effectively than that in which Valentine and Lisamon Hultin, swallowed by the dragon . . . cut their way to freedom through the creature's living flesh . . . ." [6]

Whatever else it does, *Lord Valentine's Castle* demands that its readers re-examine the relationship between science fiction and fantasy, for in this narrative Silverberg has fused the two together. [7] He broke his literary silence with an heroic quest which may serve as a model of its kind; more importantly, he created a planet which promises a wide variety of further adventures.

In a sense that in itself is the problem which *Majipoor Chronicles* (1982) faced and could not completely overcome. Silverberg attempted to contain eleven tales of unequal length—some of which have been published separately—within a narrative framework. To achieve this, he invented the boy Hissune, appointed by Lord Valentine to a clerkship in the House of Records. Instead of ancient tax records, however, Hissune has more interest in the "memory-readings" left in "the Register of Souls"; he can experience the capsules containing those memories, becoming each protagonist in turn.

The result is that *Majipoor Chronicles* simply whets the reader's appetite. Finely crafted as the stories are, they can do no more than hint at segments of Majipoor's past. Undoubtedly the most substantial story is "The Desert of Stolen Dreams" (1981), which saw both magazine and book publication. [8] In the deserts of Suvrael its protagonist, Dekkeret, seeks and unexpectedly finds relief from the overwhelming guilt which has haunted him since he allowed a companion to die unnecessarily during a hunt. He also discovers the means by which the so-called King of Dreams is able to enter the minds of sleepers. The other stories range from "Thesme and the Ghayrog" and "The Soul-Painter and the Shapeshifter," both dealing with love affairs between a human and an alien—with different results—to "The Time of the Burning," in which one of the legendary rulers ends a war with the

Metamorphs by burning a sector of land and to "Among the Dream-Speakers," in which the reader learns how Tisana, who aided Valentine in *Lord Valentine's Castle*, passed her initiation to gain her position among those who can relieve the "confusions" of human and alien alike. All of the stories, including "A Thief in Ni-moya," which reveals the fate of Inyanna, the victim of confidence men, illustrate the skill which Silverberg has shown since the beginning of his career. He is among the finest story tellers, a skilled craftsman having few equals. Thus, primarily because the *Chronicles* is a collection of shorter works, one anticipates with pleasure the long novel on which he is now working. *Valentine Pontifex*, which further opens exotic Majipoor. In that world, he has created a richly textured backdrop against which to dramatize unimagined adventures as only he can. (And this expectation ignores the promises of the historical novel, *Lord of Darkness*, whose setting has been variously described as medieval Africa and the Renaissance. Despite the label historical—perhaps because of it—one wonders whether or not it will somehow relate to the unfinished implications of *The Gate of Worlds* or will, perhaps, grow out of Silverberg's wide reading as well as his reflections upon his experiences which culminated in *Downward to the Earth*.) As one waits for these titles—as well as the many yet to be begun—perhaps the most that one can know for certain is that as Silverberg has been a major voice in contemporary fiction for the past quarter century, he will remain an outstanding contributor to the fiction of the 1980's and beyond.

NOTES

1. Clareson, "Whose Castle?: Speculations as to the Parameters of Science Ficton," *Essays in Arts and Sciences*, IX (August 1980), 140.
2. Ibid., IX, 141.
3. Silverberg, *Lord Valentine's Castle* (New York: Harper & Row, 1980), p. 325.
4. Ibid., pp. 396, 417.
5. Ibid., p. 130.
6. Clareson, "Whose Castle?," IX, 141.
7. Ibid., IX, 142.
8. Silverberg, "The Desert of Stolen Dreams," *F&SF*, 60 (June 1981), 4-47; San Francisco and Columbia, PA: Underwood-Miller, 1981 (limited edition).

SELECTED PRIMARY BIBLIOGRAPHY

For a detailed account of the first printing of Silverberg's short fiction, novels, anthologies, and non-fiction—including his pseudonymous works—and their subsequent reprintings/new editions, see my *Robert Silverberg: A Primary and Secondary Bibliography*, to be published early in 1983 by G.K. Hall & Co. The following list does not include his pseudonymous novels. For a discussion of individual stories and novels, please consult the Index.

Across A Billion Years. New York: Dial, 1969 (juvenile).

The Best of Robert Silverberg, Volume 1, New York: Pocket Books, 1976.

The Best of Robert Silverberg. Volume 2. Boston: Gregg Press, 1978.

The Book of Skulls. New York: Scribners, 1972.

Born with the Dead. New York: Random House, 1974 (three novellas).

The Calibrated Alligator. New York: Holt, Rinehart & Winston, 1969 (stories).

Capricorn Games. New York: Random House, 1976 (stories).

Conquerors from the Darkness. New York: Holt, Rinehart & Winston, 1965.

The Cube Root of Uncertainty. New York: Macmillan, 1970 (stories).

Dimension Thirteen. New York: Ballantine, 1969 (stories).

Downward to the Earth. Garden City, N.Y.: Nelson Doubleday, 1970.

Dying Inside. New York: Scribners, 1972.

Earth's Other Shadow. New York: New American Library, 1973 (stories).

The Feast of St. Dionysus. New York: Scribners, 1975 (stories).

The Gate of Worlds. New York: Holt, Rinehart & Winston, 1967 (juvenile).

Godling, Go Home. New York: Belmont, 1964 (stories).

Hawksbill Station. Garden City, N.Y.: Doubleday, 1968.

Invaders from Earth. New York: Ace Books, 1958.

Lord Valentine's Castle. New York: Harper & Row, 1980.

Lost Race of Mars. Philadelphia: Winston, 1960 (juvenile).

Majipoor Chronicles. New York: Arbor House, 1982 (stories).

The Man in the Maze. New York: Avon, 1969.

The Masks of Time. New York: Ballantine, 1968.

Master of Life and Death. New York: Ace Books, 1957.

Moonferns and Starsongs. New York: Ballantine, 1971 (stories).

Needle in a Timestack. New York: Ballantine, 1966 (stories).

Next Stop the Stars. New York: Ace Books, 1962 (stories).

Nightwings. New York: Avon, 1969.

Parsecs and Parables. Garden City, N.Y.: Doubleday, 1970 (stories).

The Planet Killers. New York: Ace Books, 1957.

Planet of Death. New York: Holt, Rinehart & Winston, 1967.

The Reality Trip. New York: Ballantine, 1972 (stories).

Recalled to Life. New York: Lancer Books, 1962; Garden City, N.Y.: Doubleday, 1972.

Regan's Planet. New York: Pyramid, 1964 (juvenile).

Revolt on Alpha C. New York: Thomas Y. Crowell, 1955 (juvenile).

The Second Trip. Garden City, N.Y.: Nelson Doubleday, 1972.

The Seed of Earth. New York: Ace Books, 1962.

The Silent Invaders. New York: Ace Books, 1959.

Son of Man. New York: Ballantine, 1971.

The Songs of Summer. London: Victor Gollancz, 1979 (stories).

"Sounding Brass, Tinkling Cymbal," in *Hell's Cartographers*. Eds. Brian W. Aldiss and Harry Harrison. London: Weidenfeld and Nicolson, 1975, pp. 7-45.

Starman's Quest. Hicksville, N.Y. Gnome Press, 1959 (juvenile).

Stepsons of Terra. New York: Ace Books, 1958.

The Stochastic Man. New York: Harper & Row, 1975.

Sundance and Other Science Fiction Stories. Nashville: Nelson, 1974 (stories).

The 13th Immortal. New York: Ace Books, 1957.

Thorns. New York: Ballantine, 1967.

Those Who Watch. New York: New American Library, 1967.

Three Survived. New York: Holt, Rinehart & Winston, 1969.

The Time-Hoppers. Garden City, N.Y.: Doubleday, 1967.

A Time of Changes. Garden City, N.Y.: Nelson Doubleday, 1971.

Time of the Great Freeze. New York: Holt, Rinehart & Winston, 1964 (juvenile).

To Open the Sky. New York: Ballantine, 1967.

To Worlds Beyond. Philadelphia: Chilton, 1965 (stories).

Tower of Glass. New York: Scribners, 1970.

Unfamiliar Territory. New York: Scribners, 1973 (stories).

Up the Line. New York: Ballantine, 1969.

Valley Beyond Time. New York: Dell, 1973 (stories).

World of a Thousand Colors. New York: Arbor House, 1982 (stories).

World's Fair, 1992. Chicago: Follet, 1970 (juvenile).

ANNOTATED SECONDARY BIBLIOGRAPHY

Clareson, Thomas D. *"Downward to the Earth,"* in *Survey of Science Fiction Literature*. Ed. Frank N. Magill. Englewood Cliffs, N.J.: Salem Press, 1979, II, 591-594. Silverberg creates a memorable character in Edmund Gundersen, who achieves transcendence through rebirth on the planet Belzagor.

_____. "The Fictions of Robert Silverberg." In *Voices for the Future*. Ed. Thomas D. Clareson. Bowling Green, Ohio: Bowling Green Popular Press, 1979, pp. 1-33. This overview stresses Silverberg's dark vision but suggests that he ranks with such writers as Coover and Barth.

_____."Introduction." *The Best of Robert Silverberg*. Boston: Gregg Press, 1978, II, vii-xxi. Stressing the short stories of the 1970's, this survey emphasizes the continuity in Silverberg's career; however, his work has grown more technically complex as he became free to write as he chose.

_____. *Robert Silverberg: A Primary and Secondary Bibliography*. Boston: G. K. Hall & Co., forthcoming for early 1983. This volume will provide a comprehensive view of the publication of Silverberg's fiction, the anthologies he has edited, his non-fiction, and his pseudonymous works. It annotates both his writings on sf and more than 700 reviews and studies of his fiction.

Currey, L. W. "Robert Silverberg." *Science Fiction and Fantasy Authors: A Bibliography of First Printings of Their Fiction*. Boston: G. K. Hall, 1979, pp. 436-438. A standard reference work, this volume gives an excellent description of Silverberg's fiction and anthologies, although confining itself to first editions only.

Edwards, Malcolm. "Robert Silverberg." In *Science Fiction Writers*. Ed. E. F. Bleiler. New York: Scribners, 1982, pp. 505-511. This is a survey of Silverberg's career, stressing the novels of the later 1960's and 1970's. If Silverberg has a "flaw," it rises from his "technical facility" making his work a "little superficial," but at its best there is an "emotional commitment to match the technique."

Gunn, James. *"Tower of Glass."* In *Survey of Science Fiction Literature*. Ed. Frank N. Magill. V, 2303-2305. This novel represents those science-fiction novels which have moved so close to the "mainstream" that it is difficult to distinguish between them. Despite its brilliance in many areas, it is an "interesting failure."

Letson, Russell. "Falling Through Many Trap Doors." *Extrapolation*, 20 (Summer 1979), 109-117. Surveying the novels of the early 1970's, Letson concludes they are structured on the theme of "anxiety" and its resolution. The constant theme in Silverberg's fiction is "pain."

_____. "Introduction," *To Open the Sky*. Boston: Gregg Press, 1977. Letson regards this work as the novel which heralded the emergence of a mature, "second" Silverberg; it develops themes and techniques dominating his fiction since 1967.

McNelly, Willis. *"Dying Inside."* In *Survey of Science Fiction Literature*. Ed. Frank N. Magill. II, 671-675. This novel is too fine a work to fall into the science-fiction category. It compares favorably with Joyce's *A Portrait of an Artist as a Young Man* and Lawrence's *Sons and Lovers*.

Reginald, Robert. "Robert Silverberg," *Science Fiction and Fantasy Literature*. Detroit: Gale Research Company, 1979, I, 476-478; II, 1074-1075. Volume one lists Silverberg's fiction and anthologies. Volume two gives a brief sketch of his career, featuring Silverberg's reflections.

Stableford, Brian M. "The Compleat Silverberg." *Speculation #31*, Autumn 1972, pp. 20-26. A survey of Silverberg's entire career concludes that his novels show his concern for human beings and, significantly, the "essential humanity" of all intelligent life-forms, however alien in appearance.

_____. *"Nightwings."* In *Survey of Science Fiction Literature*. Ed. Frank N. Magill, III, 1526-1530. The novel embodies both "empathy and pacifism" and Silverberg's central theme, the "healing of states of alienation."

_____. "Robert Silverberg." In *Science Fiction Encyclopedia*. Ed. Peter Nicholls. Garden City, N.Y. Doubleday, 1979, pp. 545-546. A brief survey of Silverberg's career concludes that "RS is one of the most imaginative and versatile" writers in the field of science fiction.

_____. *"A Time of Changes."* In *Survey of Science Fiction Literature*. Ed. Frank N. Magill, V, 2293-2297. The novel marks another of Silverberg's efforts to dramatize "situations of alienation and symbolic exorcisms thereof."

Swank, Paul. "Robert Silverberg." In *Twentieth-Century Science-Fiction Writers*. Ed. Curtis C. Smith. New York: St. Martin's Press, 1981, pp. 492-494. Devoted primarily to a listing of titles and pseudonyms, this survey discusses only a few novels in any detail. It concludes that Silverberg "is a masterful writer whose stories are always worth reading."

Tuma, George. "Robert Silverberg." In *Twentieth Century American Science-Fiction Writers*. Eds. David Cowart and Thomas L. Wymer. (*Dictionary of Literary Biography*, volume 8). Detroit: Gale Research Company, 1981, 106-119. This overview gives attention to all of Silverberg's important novels throughout his career. It concludes that he has developed into a writer producing "several works which illustrate the considerable depth and scope of his literary and philosophical concerns."

INDEX

RITTER LIBRARY
BALDWIN-WALLACE COLLEGE
WITHDRAWN